Sales Development

Sales Development

Cory Bray and Hilmon Sorey

Foreword by Chris Beall
Afterword by Ryan Reisert

ISBN: 1979107947
ISBN-13: 9781979107945
Library of Congress Control Number: 2017919189
CreateSpace Independent Publishing Platform
North Charleston, South Carolina

Contents

Foreword

How could I resist accepting the invitation from Cory and Hilmon to write a foreword to "Sales Development"? This deep truth, found in Chapter 1, would have convinced me all by itself:

> As companies moved to a SaaS model and it became easier for buyers to purchase and implement software, vendors realized that the number of conversations salespeople were having was the factor limiting revenue. In other words, "the more conversations we have, the more money we make!"

But I had a little baggage to overcome. You see, I started out as a Sales Development skeptic back in 2011 when I found myself working at ConnectAndSell, a sales technology company. The company's product delivers targeted conversations very quickly, and it seemed obvious to me – still does, actually – that senior salespeople, and even more senior executives, should have more conversations with their prospects and customers.

Then I woke up and smelled the silence. It turns out that no matter how easy you make it, people are generally afraid of having conversations with invisible strangers. It makes sense when you think about it from a historical, or pre-historical, perspective: that unfamiliar voice calling from the dark woods at the edge of your village at midnight is almost certainly more dangerous than a tiger, or even a snake in the tall grass.

And all customers start out as strangers, and are almost always invisible – because they are far away, not because of some weird superpower. So, to echo Professor Clayton Christensen, we have a "Job To Be Done" – a job that starts with having conversations with invisible strangers.

This scary job is essential, especially for Software as a Service (SaaS) companies, who must turn a lot of those strangers into customers before the money runs out. And what do we do when we have a "Job To Be Done" that is scary? We specialize, partly because the job is important, and partly because you can get used to doing something scary if you do it over and over.

The Sales Development Rep, or SDR, is exactly that specialist. And like any good specialty, this one requires a special mix of skills, attitude, situation and relationships to be worth the cost, effort and handoff risks that come with specializing. Specialists need, among other things, a handbook: a body of organized knowledge they can turn to time and again to guide them in preparing for, managing or recovering from the inevitable challenges they will face.

"Sales Development" is precisely that handbook. My recommendation is to read it through once if your professional life touches modern sales in any way. Or, frankly, if you have a daughter, son, spouse or friend who is either in Sales Development, or thinking about making the plunge. Your first read will give you a sense of what it's all about and some strong hints about where you should focus your attention.

But the first read through is only the beginning, especially if you decide to embark on a sales career starting as an SDR – regardless of whether you have a burning desire to become an Account Executive, a Professional SDR, or CEO for that matter. This is a handbook. Keep it with you, electronically or otherwise. Refer to it. Re-read the relevant chapters at the right time.

This book covers everything, from getting hired to moving on, from phone to email to text to social, from how to manage your time to how to work with your "clients" (Account Executives) and various bosses. It's detailed, down-to-earth, reality based and truly instructional.

In other words, there's a Job To Be Done. Time to get on with it.

Chris Beall

Introduction

Chapter Goal: Gain a high-level understanding of the sales development role and determine how you can use this book to accelerate your career!

*I*t was a brisk fall day, and we just finished a meeting with Alex at a restaurant in San Francisco. She picked up the tab, checked her phone to ensure her flight was on time, and thanked us for providing helpful insights on such short notice as she dashed out the door to catch a plane from SFO to New York. She was set to interview two candidates for a sales development manager position in one of three offices she now manages as director of sales for a hot San Francisco–based tech company.

We first met Alex a few years earlier. She was a wide-eyed recent college grad with a liberal arts degree and a desire to move to the Bay Area to work in tech. We were helping to grow the sales team at a start-up, and part of that engagement included performing initial interviews with candidates like Alex. She had no sales expertise beyond recruiting members for her college sorority and raising money from alumni...but she had a ton of passion.

This time she wanted advice on hiring methodologies for sales development managers. Next time, we will probably discuss the systems, key performance indicators, and growth metrics necessary to scale her team globally. The time after that, we'll likely be discussing the new start-up she's founded and how to go about raising capital.

We worked with Alex from her initial hire as a sales development rep through to her growth to account executive, then to manager, then to director. There is a science to her success. Sure, there is a bit of luck, but she positioned herself to seize opportunity whenever it was offered.

Sales development is the entry point to the fast track of sales. It requires a "certain set of skills," a commitment to activity, a knowledge foundation upon which to grow, and a repeatable process to beat the pack. We have cultivated individual success and have grown teams by working with sales development representatives (SDRs), managers, and the executive leadership of organizations that range from start-ups to Fortune 50. In this book, we have distilled the key elements of sales development to position you for success in this role and beyond.

What Is Sales, and Why Does It Matter?

In any company, sales is the department that generates revenue. No matter how good your manufacturing operation is, how cutting-edge your technology might be, or how progressive and forward-thinking your management techniques are, you must still have a sales mechanism in place, or else everything else is useless.

What Are SaaS Companies?

You might not know what SaaS means, but you have heard of companies who follow this business model. Salesforce.com started the SaaS revolution, and since then, most software products are offered "as a service," or SaaS.

In the old days, people used to buy on-premises software, meaning that they would physically install CDs onto their servers. With the advent of the cloud, the SaaS model was born, and companies no longer had to deal with the costs of on-premises software.

What Is a Sales Development Rep (SDR)?

As companies moved to a SaaS model and it became easier for buyers to purchase and implement software, vendors realized that the number of conversations salespeople were having was the factor limiting revenue. In other words, the more conversations we have, the more money we make!

One challenge is that most SaaS companies are not profitable and therefore need to invest their cash very wisely. Instead of having highly paid account executives (AEs) opening *and* closing deals, companies started hiring SDRs to create opportunities for AEs to close, as shown in figure 0.1.

Once the SDR speaks with a prospect, the prospect is identified either as not a good fit and is disqualified, or as someone who might make a good customer and is passed on to the AE, who will qualify, demo, and close the deal! Passing a lead is also commonly referred to as "creating an opportunity," with SDRs handling "leads" and AEs handling "opportunities."

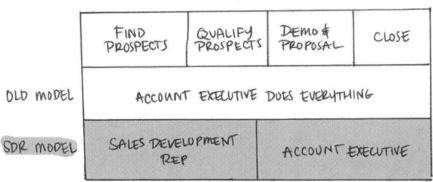

Figure 0.1: Adding SDRs creates specialization on the sales team.

Market Outlook for SDRs

The market is hot! Sales development is a rapidly growing role that has moved beyond tech and is now popular in non-venture-backed organizations as well. Companies are building SDR teams and expanding the ones they already have in place.

There is even an annual Sales Development Conference in San Francisco, another sign that the market for the role is on fire.

Compensation Ranges for SDRs

We recently heard of an SDR who made more than $40,000 in a *quarter*! We know many who have earned more than $100,000 in a year. Yes, SDRs can make a lot of money!

Depending on the market, base salaries can range from $30,000 to $65,000+, and hitting quota typically results in a payday of 1.4× to 1.6× that number. There are also accelerator bonuses that allow you to earn exponentially more money for each opportunity you create after hitting quota.

Backgrounds Appropriate for an SDR

A wide range of individuals have become SDRs, as the position does not require one specific type of work experience and may not require any at all. People who perform the best, however, typically have the following attributes:

*   **Fearless**: Talking to strangers and being told no thirty times in a row is not a big deal.
*   **Articulate**: Excellent command of language and ability to speak in a professional tone.
*   **Driven**: The goal isn't to hit quota...it's to *crush* quota!
*   **Curious**: By talking 30 percent of the time and asking a lot of questions, prospects' needs are well understood.

If these attributes sound like you, you're in the right place!

Who Should Read This Book?

Sales development reps can explore what we have written to see if there is an opportunity to improve their performance in their current role and also better plan their career.

Sales development managers can strengthen their understanding of what sets a great SDR apart from the crowd.

Account executives wishing to get inside the head of the modern SDR can use topics from this book to initiate conversations with their colleagues and help drive better lead flow.

Sales leaders can ensure that their team is focused on the right things and is taking advantage of the tactics we outline. We recommend that sales leaders also read *The Sales Development Playbook* by Trish Bertuzzi.

How to Use This Book

Each chapter follows a similar structure, with summary content at both the beginning and the end.

>**Chapter Goal:** Each chapter will begin with a summary of what you will learn.

>**Awesome Alex:** We profile a fictional SDR named "Awesome" Alex through each chapter. Following the Chapter Goal, we tell a quick story of how Alex has used various principles to become a top performer. Many of these stories were inspired by real events we have observed. She is accompanied by some of her colleagues, including:

>>**Lazy Leonard**—Puts in little effort and cannot hit quota.

>>**Feature-Loving Fran**—Thinks prospects buy because of features.

>>**Tool-Happy Terri**—Wants to automate everything.

>>**Distracted Dino**—Too busy to focus and do his job.

>**Content:** The bulk of each chapter. Here you will find a combination of theoretical concepts and actionable tactics to

improve your performance. We use several diagrams and a lot of bullet points to make the information as digestible as possible.

Maximillian's Mishaps: Learning from others' mistakes is one of the smartest things you can do in sales development and business in general. Our fictional character, Maximillian, might be the worst SDR in history. Learn from his mishaps so you don't repeat them yourself.

Boss's Brain: Want to get inside your boss's head and see what he or she really cares about? Here's your chance!

Additional Material: You can find more information on our website, SalesDevelopmentBook.com.

Chapter 1

• • •

Getting the Job

Chapter Goal: You will have the knowledge and skills to identify great job opportunities, secure interviews, and receive offers from top companies.

Alex is the top SDR at ExampleCorp, one of the hottest companies in the United States. A little over a year ago, she wasn't. Heck, she didn't even have a job, and she wasn't getting any responses from the applications she was sending to potential employers. Armed with a liberal arts degree and a ton of ambition, Alex was trying to figure out what she wanted to do next, and she started to notice that a lot of her most successful friends were working in sales.

With the help of a mentor, she was able to find a company hiring SDRs in a hot market that was highly respected by customers and employees. She quickly landed an interview and crushed the hiring process. At every step, she had a good idea of what she was going to be asked and was armed with responses that left heads nodding in agreement. She also knew about the red flags hiring managers look for and how to avoid doing anything that could disqualify her as a candidate.

Alex mastered the skill of landing a job in sales development, and now you can too!

Types of Sales Organizations

One of the first considerations when looking for a job is the size and stage of company where you want to work. Figure 1.1 highlights the difference between size and stage at a high level.

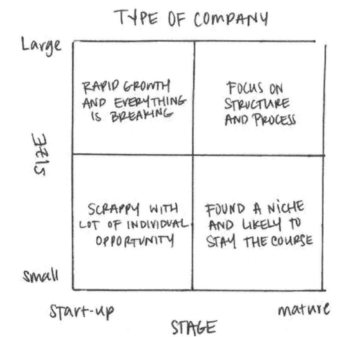

Figure 1.1: Companies operate differently depending on their size and stage.

Sales Development

We broke this diagram into four quadrants for simplicity, but in reality, each axis is a spectrum with many points along the way.

Let's first look at company stage:

Start-up: An early stage company that is either just getting its first sales or has had success in a small number of niche markets. You will have direct access to executives, but formal training is probably lacking, and a high level of resourcefulness and resilience will be required.

Growth: Companies enter this stage when they have an established a repeatable sales process. There is strong demand for their product, so adding more salespeople directly results in more revenue. Strong executives are hired here, so this stage is where you find top-tier mentors, clear process, and high velocity.

Mature: The quick wins are in the rearview mirror, and focus shifts to operational efficiency and potentially bigger, more complex deals. Process and structure are valued, though creativity can still be applied to how specific deals are managed. You can learn a lot, but the company likely won't change very much unless it is acquired.

Now let's examine company size:

Small (<100 employees): You will have more direct access to executives, and there is likely a "just-get-it-done" attitude with little bureaucracy.

Medium (100–1,000 employees): Process becomes necessary to accelerate growth and create predictability, so managers are hired to control chaos and scale the organization.

Large (>1,000 employees): Layers of management are necessary to maintain control of many moving parts that might exist in multiple product lines, multiple offices, different markets, and various internal departments.

The last two variables to consider are the company's financing (venture capital or bootstrapped) and ownership structure (public or private).

Venture-Backed: Rapidly spend money and focus on growth. If milestones are not hit every eighteen to thirty-six months, the company will die.

Bootstrapped: Focused on stability and profitability first and then growth. These companies can grow fast, but not as fast as if they were venture-backed.

Public: Stock trades on a major exchange, and quarterly earnings reports impact stock price.

Privately Held: Private investors hold the stock. While quarterly numbers are important to the board of directors, there is more flexibility to take risks and make long-term investments than if they were public.

Major SDR Functions

There are three major distinctions between SDR functions that you should understand before looking for a job:

* Where do the leads come from?
* What do I do with the leads?
* How much research is required?

If you map each of these points against your strengths and then interview for jobs that align the best, you are more likely to land somewhere you will be happy.

Inbound versus Outbound

Inbound SDRs will call leads who have expressed interest in your company. These prospects may have:

* given their contact information in exchange for a white paper, case study, analyst report, or another asset that they perceived valuable;
* requested a demo;
* visited your booth at a trade show or attended another in-person event.

Outbound SDRs will reach out to cold prospects from a list of target accounts.

Both roles will speak with and qualify prospects. Also, when inbound leads dry up, everyone becomes an outbound SDR. Companies do not pay you to sit there and wait for leads.

Appointment Setting versus Qualifying

In an appointment-setting role, your sole goal is to coordinate a meeting between the prospect and your AE. You might do so over e-mail or phone, with the only goal being to schedule the next conversation.

In a qualifying role, there are questions to satisfy that determine whether it makes sense to introduce the prospect to an AE. We cover some of these questions in the "Sales Methodology" section of chapter 2.

While it's perfectly fine to set appointments for a short period of time, this type of role is significantly constrained. Simply setting appointments via email does not create a compelling professional development opportunity.

The Amount of Research and Outreach

Will you spend a lot of your time researching prospects and creatively uncovering leads? Or is research fairly automated or performed elsewhere in the organization so you can focus on calling, e-mailing, and social selling? SDR research focuses on identifying:

* who to talk to;
* how to reach them;
* what to talk about.

If you don't love research and want to get on the phone, find companies where SDRs can sit down and get to prospecting without having to do a bunch of prework. It's important to know how to research, but if that's what you wanted to do all day, you would probably be applying for analyst roles, not reading a book on sales development.

What Companies Are Looking for in an SDR

Employers want people who can feed sales pipelines today and become the leaders of tomorrow. Additionally, they want people who can execute an activity plan, learn quickly, "figure it out," maintain accountability, are team players, and match their company culture.

Getting Started
Clean Up Your Social Media
Being reckless with social media will kill your interview process before it starts. Always apply the "Grandmother Test":

> *Are you willing to sit next to your grandmother and show her this picture or post? If not, delete it.*

Sure, drinking is legal. Dressing like an idiot (usually) won't get you arrested. Some states even let you smoke pot! However, what does your future manager see when a picture of you holding a beer and smoking a joint while wearing a chicken suit pops up on Facebook?

The person who hires you is accountable for your success and has his or her own career aspirations. If you do something stupid at a company event, are slow to ramp, or otherwise don't "fit in," and this behavior could have been predicted based on your social media posts, the person who hired you will have some explaining to do.

How to Research Companies and Hiring Managers
Accepting a job is a big decision and should not be taken lightly. In this section, we cover several attributes to examine when evaluating a potential employer. We have provided a framework in figure 1.2.

Before you start looking at specific companies, think about what you want and what you are willing to sacrifice across each of these categories. Maybe you care most about finding a really strong

CATEGORY	WHAT I WANT	I WILL SACRIFICE	SCORE 1-BAD 5-GOOD
SALES DEVELOPMENT LEADERSHIP			
EXECUTIVE LEADERSHIP			
EMPLOYEE HAPPINESS			
CUSTOMER HAPPINESS			
MARKET CONDITIONS			
TOTAL SCORE:			

Figure 1.2: Satisfaction scorecard for job seekers.

leadership team, and it's OK if other employees complain about long hours and lots of stress. Begin with the end in mind.

As you research companies and begin to participate in interviews, scoring them along the way can help ensure you end up in the best possible situation.

Evaluate Sales Development Leadership

The best thing you can do for your long-term career is to work for great bosses. You will learn a tremendous amount over time, and if you work together well, they will become lifelong advocates for your career.

While many types of people can be a good boss, when looking for a job, it's key to find someone who can help advance your career far and fast. In figure 1.3 we look at two areas where sales development leaders can be evaluated: work experience and the management training they have received.

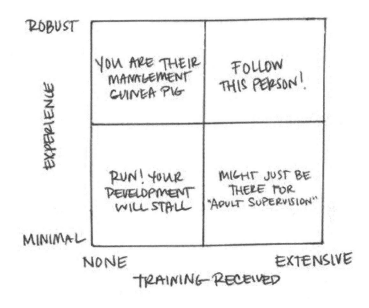

Figure 1.3: Identify great managers based on work experience and training.

Minimal Experience, No Training: These people were likely SDRs within the last few years and were then promoted to manager. They will be a huge help to you for a short while, but soon you will have an overlapping skill set, and they won't have the management skills to help develop you further.

Robust Experience, No Training: People who have likely worked in several sales organizations and have great experience. However, without management training, they are likely to say "do it like I do," which is not an ideal way for you to develop your skill set.

Minimal Experience, Extensive Training: Sometimes companies hire "adult supervision," which means experienced managers to oversee groups where they have no functional expertise. If the experienced managers have the desire to jump in and really learn the job, that's great, but if they want to sit behind their computer and go to meetings all day, you have a high-paid babysitter.

Robust Experience, Extensive Training: The holy grail! These people understand the job and know how to develop you into a rock star! They have solid sales experience, have been formally trained in management, and also likely have amazing mentors. These are the types of leaders you want to find!

You can learn about their experience from LinkedIn and start to glean insights into their management skills from public review sites like Glassdoor. Once you get an interview, asking about the management training the leadership team has received is a great question. If they are in the upper-right quadrant of figure 1.3, they will happily brag about it and will be glad you asked.

Evaluate Sales and Executive Leadership
Sales leaders and senior executives often make several hundred thousand dollars each year and sometimes millions. Do you know why?

Successful executives can build teams that win predictably, and companies pay big bucks for that!

When these leaders view you as an invaluable resource, it creates a symbiotic relationship. They need to build a team, and you follow them because you know they will win...then eventually you can become

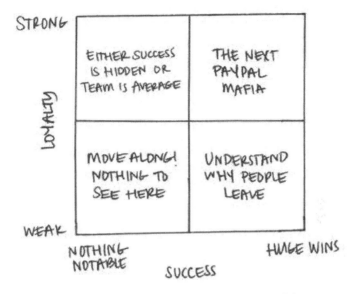

STRONG

LOYALTY

EITHER SUCCESS IS HIDDEN OR TEAM IS AVERAGE

THE NEXT PAYPAL MAFIA

MOVE ALONG! NOTHING TO SEE HERE

UNDERSTAND WHY PEOPLE LEAVE

WEAK

NOTHING NOTABLE

HUGE WINS

SUCCESS

Figure 1.4: Strong executive leadership will have prior success and loyal employees.

more and more like them. Two attributes that can be used to identify these leaders are highlighted in figure 1.4 and discussed below.

Weak Loyalty, Little Success: These leaders might have real potential, but they haven't realized it yet, and employees are not sticking around to see what happens. Red flag.

Weak Loyalty, Huge Success: People are either leaving because they are getting hired to build their own teams (great outcome), or the executive team is toxic and bad to work with (bad outcome). Also, realize that acquisitions for an amount that was not publicly disclosed[1] does not indicate success.

---

1 When a company is acquired for "an undisclosed amount," you should do additional research to ensure it was not a failure.

Strong Loyalty, Little Success: Private company success is not always public, so there might be hidden information somewhere. Alternatively, the team might be mediocre and have limited options to go elsewhere.

Strong Loyalty, Huge Success: This is where you want to be! If the executives are moving their team from company to company and winning, you want to join the movement!

The PayPal Mafia is an example of a team of high-performing people who worked together and have since gone on to accomplish amazing things. Apply rigor and research to your job search, and you will significantly increase your chances of identifying a successful opportunity that has huge long-term upside.

Employee Happiness

Before getting excited about a company, go check out the reviews on Glassdoor.com, where employees give feedback on their companies and executives. If the employees who work there today aren't happy, how will that change when you arrive?

Most importantly, read the details of the negative reviews. These will give you insights into what it's really like to work at the company.

Be wary of clusters of five-star reviews that follow negative posts. Sometimes this activity points to company manipulation. A positive review without detailed comments isn't helpful and should be discounted.

In addition to reading online, it also helps to reach out to current and former employees. If you ask for confidential feedback on what it's like to work at the company, most people will be honest since they feel like you're making a big life decision partially based on their input.

Customer Happiness

Here's what will happen if you work at a company that has unhappy customers:

*   Unhappy customers will leave, which will reduce your company's revenue, eventually causing financial challenges.
*   Unhappy customers will talk about their feelings publicly; then your competitors will amplify this conversation, making it harder to sell your product.
*   Your top salespeople will quit once it's hard to sell the product, which will lead to other top employees quitting, and all of a sudden your team is full of mediocre performers.

Market Conditions

When it comes to the market, the most important principle is:

A rising tide floats all boats.

When market conditions are right, you and all of your competitors can do great. The pie is getting bigger, and everyone can have a significant slice. Here are the metrics to evaluate market conditions:

*   **Quota Attainment**: Are most SDRs hitting quota, while some are making 200–300 percent?
*   **Recent Catalyst**: Has an event (like a consolidation, regulation, deregulation, or innovation) caused an increased demand for the product?

* **Runway**: How much opportunity is left in the market? Is the well about to run dry?

If you get into the right company with the right boss, you will be in great shape. If you also have the right market, amazing things will happen.

Approaching Your Target Companies
"Prospecting" into Potential Employers

As an SDR, your job will be to reach out to prospective customers who might have a problem you can solve.

Well, if someone is hiring an SDR, what a better opportunity to show that you can walk the walk? Here are some tactics you can use to show off your skills:

* **Go Omni-Channel**: Use the tools you will leverage as an SDR, including the phone, e-mail, social, and video.
* **Call High**: Even if the internal recruiter posted the job, reach out to the VP of sales.
* **Add Value**: Bring an idea showing how adding you to the team would be transformative.
* **Set Next Steps**: When you connect with someone, be prepared to close them on a next step.

Managers are very concerned with de-risking their hiring decision. They need to truly believe:

If I hire this person, there is an excellent chance that he or she will be successful.

What better way to help managers de-risk their decisions than doing the exact thing they're hiring you for during the recruiting process?

Applying Online versus Getting a Referral

Once you're an SDR, do you expect to send your prospect one e-mail and hope to get a response? We're still early in the book, but here's a hint...that won't work unless you get lucky! It typically takes several attempts to get a prospect's attention, and e-mail-only strategies don't work anymore.

Applying online is the job seeker's equivalent of sending one e-mail to a prospect and hoping he or she wants to meet.

It might be tricky to get a referral, especially to small companies, but here are some ideas you can try:

First-Degree Connections: If you know someone who works there, have a conversation about your interest in the job and ask for an introduction to the hiring manager.

Second-Degree Connections: Use LinkedIn to see if some-one you know is connected to someone at the company.

Connect Online: Engage with social posts by commenting in a thoughtful manner to get noticed.

Connect Offline: Find out where people who work at the company will be in person and meet them there. You might find them at a trade show, meetup, or another event.

Whatever you do, don't be a stalker. Any creepy or overly aggressive behavior will kill your chances on the spot.

Working with Recruiters

There are two basic types of recruiters:

In-House: Employees who work for one specific company.

Agency: Independent contractors who work with many companies at once.

In-house recruiters are presented with open job requisitions for multiple departments inside of a company. Their job is both to source and manage the talent pipeline for each position. Their role involves initial screening, interview scheduling, assessments (sometimes), obtaining references, conducting background checks, presenting offers, and ultimately closing candidates. Depending on the organization, this can be a high-volume and/or high-velocity role with a significant amount of pressure. They may work with product development, engineering, marketing, sales, and other departments to fill roles with the best people.

Keys to working with in-house recruiters include:

* **Be highly responsive** to all inquiries.
* **Keep your appointments**, but if you are unable to do so, give plenty of advance notice so that you do not embarrass a recruiter by wasting an executive's time.
* **Be honest** about your background, capabilities, and interest in the position.

* **Provide feedback** relevant to your conversations at each stage of the process, and ask any questions you may have as they arise.

Agency recruiters are hired to fill jobs for multiple companies. Their focus is to constantly network, source, and cultivate qualified candidates for roles at client companies. The best recruiters have a consistent pipeline of qualified, interested, and high-performing candidates. If you fit this profile, they want to meet you! Just remember that they work for their clients, not specifically for you, and they are likely working with several other candidates.

When working with a recruiter, here are some questions you should consider asking:

* Why has the position become available?
* What are the main objectives and responsibilities of the position?
* How does the company expect these objectives to be met?
* What are the measures used to judge how successful I am in the role?
* What obstacles are commonly encountered in reaching these objectives?
* What can I expect in terms of development and support?
* Where will the job fit into the team structure?
* What is the company culture like?

The Phone Screen

The phone screen is the first step in an organization's interaction with candidates and allows for an individual to quickly interact with a large number of candidates in a small amount of time. Keep in mind that the job of an SDR requires a significant amount of time on the phone, so do not take this step lightly.

As you prepare for the interview, here are some tips to consider:

* **Make a cheat sheet!** Review the job description and any notes you have been provided by the post, recruiter, or individual who set up the phone screen.
* **Prepare questions.** Write down any questions you may want to ask—before you get on the phone. Be sure to ask what the next steps will be.
* **Chill out**. Here's a hint: this is much easier to do the more opportunities you have.

Additionally, make sure you are ready for the mechanics of the call:

* Answer the phone yourself.
* Ensure that you are in a place with no background noise and good reception.
* Make sure your phone is charged.
* Be on time.
* Let the interviewer finish the question before answering.

What to Expect During the Interview

Phone interviews can vary from the sophisticated to the incredibly amateur. At the sophisticated end of the spectrum, you should be prepared for interviewers to act much like a prospect would on the phone: curt, abrupt, detached, a bit apathetic. Why are they doing that? To see how you respond to what might become your everyday job! If you are easily flustered or noticeably "hurt," then the interviewer may conclude that you don't have the stomach for an SDR role.

You might also be asked to explain your background, why you applied for the position, or even walk through your resume. Imagine again that you are speaking with a prospect. Be clear, concise, and conversational. We've heard nervous candidates take up eight minutes of a ten-minute interview in a soliloquy about their college life. Practice what you will say and keep it tight.

You are being evaluated on your ability to establish rapport with the interviewer as well. Does it feel like a conversation, or are you just playing tennis with questions that are volleyed your way? Are you showing enthusiasm? Are you engaging on the phone, or do you sound boring?

Here's an idea...why don't you role-play a phone interview with a friend and record yourself? It's a ten-minute exercise that could make or break your career chances.

Closing the Next Conversation

Remember that the phone screen is the first step of a process. There is no need to try to get a job offer here. You are only looking to close the next step, which is likely an in-person interview. Here are some tips to close the next step:

*   **Ask what happens next** and when. However, if you are no longer interested, this is the time when you can exit the interview process.

* **Send a follow-up e-mail** thanking the interviewer for his or her time and reiterating any salient points from the conversation.
* **Cloze the loop** with the recruiter. Immediately make him or her aware of any commitments made or what you learned about the process, including interviewer feedback.

A follow-up e-mail might look something like this:

[Interviewer Name],

It was great speaking with you today! After learning more about [Company Name], I'm more excited than ever. The team sounds amazing, the market is very interesting, and I believe that I can make a significant impact.

Thanks again! I'm looking forward to our next steps.

[Signature]

The On-Site Interview Process
Dress

It's sad that we even have to cover this topic, but apparently, not everyone knows how to dress for job interviews. We recently heard a story where someone wore a tracksuit to an interview, "because it was inside sales."

While we love Tracksuit Tuesday, Flannel Friday, and other fun traditions, the interview is not the time for theme dress...do that after you have an offer in hand. Very simply, dress how you would if you were meeting with a prospect in real life. In most cases, that's business casual, but use your judgment.

Preparation—Different from the Phone Screen

If you *really* want the job, on interview day, you should know enough to jump into an SDR's chair and start making calls. After all, we recommend that SDRs are on the phone day two at the latest!

Some areas you might want to prepare for include:

* **SDR Skills**: Being conversational about what you will do on the job will reduce a lot of the risk for hiring managers. This book should put you in a good place.
* **Their Customers**: Know their big customers and why they bought, including the problem they were solving and how things worked out. Case studies on their website will give you this information.
* **Buyer Personas**: Who are the specific people who buy and use the product and why?
* **Their Product**: What does it do? What problem does it solve? So what?
* **The Market**: What is their market in general? Who are the competitors and what is your company's advantage?

Mastering the points above will put you in the top tier of SDR candidates.

Posture

While yes, we do mean "don't slouch," more importantly we mean the attitude you demonstrate while interacting in a business context. Do you present as someone who will be comfortable in conversation with prospects? Or do you wilt a bit when speaking to people who may be senior to you? Would an executive find you credible, articulate, curious, insightful, and mature? Interviewers will be making either formal or mental notes about each of these criteria.

What to Expect

In sophisticated companies, the interview process is highly choreographed. Specific individuals will ask specific questions at specific times, and each person will keep score in a rubric similar to the one shown in figure 1.5. Everyone's scores will be tallied at the end and will play a key role in the decision process.

CANDIDATE	POSTURE	TECH SAVVY	CLARITY	CURIOSITY	RESOURCEFULNESS
PERSON A					
PERSON B					
YOU					

Figure 1.5: A preview of how companies will score you during interviews.

Other companies are a little less formal and may "grab whoever is available" for your interview. In addition to the hiring manager, you might speak with one of his or her peers, a senior team member, or even someone from a different department.

The key to remember is that you want to take every opportunity to reflect your competency and capability *relevant to the specifics outlined in the job description.* If you build model trains as a hobby, there is no point in talking about it unless you are aligning the patience, research, and detail-oriented planning it takes for you to lay tracks to the those necessary to be an effective SDR at the company where you are interviewing.

In a less formal interview process, you may find yourself being asked the same questions over and over again. Every time you answer should be fresh like the first time you were asked! Also be aware of coaching tips. We've advised hiring managers to suggest things like:

> Pat, who you'll meet in the next interview, likes to hear about how mentors have impacted candidates' growth throughout their lives.

Guess what you better be prepared to do when you speak with Pat? This tactic is often an attempt to uncover whether or not you are coachable.

Keep in mind that the hiring process is expensive for companies (add all the hours required of everyone involved times the number of interviews, figure in the conversion ratio of interviewees to hires, and you get a ton of money) and the interview process is seldom set up to be punitive or involve trickery. Smart companies want an opportunity for their hiring managers and candidates alike to qualify or disqualify for an opportunity to work together in the most transparent way possible.

Most interviewers are hoping that you will be that perfect candidate...so they can get back work!

Group Interviews

Group interviews are an opportunity to expedite the interview process, understand how you perform under a little pressure, and give multiple individuals an opportunity to interact with you. In a group interview, be sure to include everyone. Make eye contact with all parties regardless of your perception of hierarchy.

Off-Site Interview (Lunch, Coffee, Happy Hour)

Employers often look for an opportunity to get candidates out of the office and away from the formality of the interview process. Here you have a chance to see how well you will fit with company culture and what you're like as a person. This is a great time to be yourself (on your best behavior).

Do we have to say "don't get wasted," "don't argue," and "don't evangelize on controversial topics"?

Be cool, yo. You're almost there! Be inquisitive. You have an opportunity to learn about the people you will work with and vice versa. If they are taking the time to hang out with you, chances are they are committed to their company and maintaining its culture.

Full-Day Shadowing

Shadowing means following around someone who would be your peer for a day. It's a chance for you to see what the job is really like. It's also a chance for them to see what you are really like.

If you are invited to shadow an existing employee for a day, that's a great sign! It means they want to be sure that the things you've claimed in an interview and on your resume are actually things you are capable of doing! Don't be a wallflower or passively watch while trying to stay out of the way. Be inquisitive. Demonstrate comprehension of what you are being shown. If you can help—then do so! Set up the framework from the very beginning.

Stacey, I appreciate the chance to shadow you today and learn more about the role. Is there anything in particular I can help you with today? Will it be OK for me to ask a ton of questions? Is there anything in particular you're hoping to learn about me?

Why guess at these things? Find a way to add value while figuring out if you still want the job. Turn your phone off and dig in!

Closing the Job

The best way to close a job is to be clear about expected outcomes at the very beginning.

When the on-site interview is being scheduled, ask the recruiter or manager what you should expect and what the next steps will be if the interviews are successful. As a salesperson, you will begin to understand that getting agreement on next steps is an essential means of moving a process forward in an honest and transparent way. When you have managed next steps throughout the process, closing activity simply involves you restating your interest (and the reasons why you think you are a strong fit for the opportunity) and asking for the position.

Sam, I want to thank you and the team for the interview process. I appreciate you answering my questions, and I learned a lot. I'm convinced that based on my passion for the security industry, experience in data mining and research, persistence, and resourcefulness, I could hit the ground running in this SDR role. I learn quickly and would love to work here. What are your thoughts?

Yup. Just that easy.

What is Backchanneling?

You will be asked for references toward the end of the interview process, but savvy employers will also reach out to others you have worked with in the past. This process is called "backchanneling," and provides additional insights beyond your handpicked references who (hopefully) like you.

If you have beef with an old boss, try to make things right before it costs you a job. Life is too short to be beefing with people.

Stupid Moves People Make

Here are some dumb things that Maximillian would say in the interview process:

* Do you allow dogs?
* What are the work hours?
* How much vacation do I get?
* When will I get promoted?

Maximillian also likes to talk at length about his life experiences, which have little relevance to the position for which he is applying.

If you are applying to work at a company with an existing SDR team, all of these points have been worked out, and asking for change can have you come across as being difficult.

If you really want to know the answer to any of these questions, subtly ask someone who works there or have your friend do it...don't ask management.

The Offer

Sales offers are like no other. Your compensation package will contain many components, such as:

* **Base Salary**: The amount you will be paid every pay period, regardless of performance.
* **Variable Compensation**: Performance-related compensation that could be paid monthly, quarterly, or annually.
* **Spiffs**: Short-term incentives that might not be explicitly called out in the offer letter.
* **Equity**: Ownership in the company.

We have included a sample offer letter in appendix A for your review.

On-Target Earnings (OTE)

Your OTE is the amount you will earn if you hit your goals (also known as quota). One of the best parts of sales roles is that you're able to earn well above your OTE if you do well. While compensation varies by industry, here's an example of how OTE might be calculated:

* **Base Salary**: Fixed amount you earn for showing up.
* **Leads Qualified**:
    * $0 if you qualify <30 per month.
    * $125 per lead up to 40 per month.
    * $200 per lead for each one over 40.
* **Revenue**: 0.5 percent of revenue closed for any deal where you hit your lead quota.

In general, SDRs are paid 50–70 percent base salary and 30–50 percent variable compensation if they hit quota. Obviously, someone who exceeds quota can make much more money…which is why sales is exciting!

What is Equity and How Does It Work?

Equity (also referred to as stock) represents a fractional ownership stake in your company. As an SDR, you will likely receive stock options, which mean you have the right to buy a certain amount of stock at a certain price (called the "strike price"). These options are "granted" to you when you commence employment, but you don't actually own them until they "vest." Most companies offer equity that vests over four years with a one-year cliff. That means:

* You own nothing until you reach your one-year anniversary (the cliff), at which point you own 25 percent of the original option grant.
* After the one-year cliff, your equity vests monthly in equal increments, so with each month that passes, you own another one forty-eighth of the grant.

Just because you vested, however, doesn't mean you can sell. There is no market for private company stock, and employees of public companies might still have some restrictions on when they can sell.

If you do sell, you will "exercise the option" by buying it for the strike price at which it was granted and then sell for the market price.

*Profit = (Market Price - Strike Price) * Number of Shares*

If the market price is below the exercise price, the option is worthless, so you would not exercise.

Finally, many companies require you to exercise your options within a short time after your employment terminates, or else they will be forfeited. If you have 10,000 vested options at a strike price of $2.00, you will need to pay $20,000 to exercise the options or you will lose them forever. If your company is still private, you might not be able to sell this stock for a long time, so the decision to exercise weighs heavily on your risk tolerance and belief in the company's ability to be successful.

Finding Comparables

In addition to being a resource for employee reviews, Glassdoor.com also provides information on compensation. You can see what SDRs are paid at the company, and if they don't have any info, you can at least see what others are making while working in similar roles in your city.

Negotiating Compensation

If you are the first or second SDR at a company and the compensation plan seems out of whack, you might have some room to negotiate. However, as with other junior-level jobs, there likely isn't much wiggle room. If you take the offer and do a great job, you will be fairly compensated in the long run.

A Basic Negotiating Framework

Let's now introduce a framework (figure 1.6) that can be used for negotiating compensation, but also serves as the foundation for

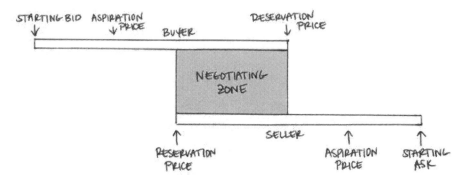

Figure 1.6: A negotiating framework that can be
used for job offers or closing deals.

negotiating deals with prospects. In this case, the "buyer" is the
company hiring, and the "seller" is the candidate looking for a job.

In any negotiation, the buyer and seller both have:

* **An Aspiration Price**: The ideal price each party will accept
  (high for the seller and low for the buyer).
* **A Reservation Price**: The worst price either party will accept
  (low for the seller and high for the buyer).
* **The Best Alternative to a Negotiated Agreement (BATNA)**:
  If a deal doesn't happen, this is where things stand.
* **Starting Bid**: Buyers will initially offer to pay less than their
  aspiration price.
* **Starting Ask**: Sellers will initially ask for more than their as-
  piration price.

The area where the distance between the aspiration and reservation prices for both the buyer and the seller overlap is known as
the "Negotiating Zone." In this zone, any deal can get done if both

parties can find their ways to a common number. Outside of this zone, there will be no deal, and the BATNA becomes the reality.

Maximillian's Mishaps

* Talks about politics when looking for a job. Whatever he says will alienate half of the people he meets.
* Fields phone interviews wherever it's convenient: at coffee shops, on public transportation, or in the living room with his roommates watching professional wrestling.
* Shows up more than five minutes early for an interview and lurks around in the reception area. Or worse...he shows up late.
* Sends texts and keeps his social media up-to-date during "shadow day."
* Takes the first job offer he gets, even if he doesn't love the opportunity. (You wouldn't marry the first person you met on Tinder!)
* Ignores the fact that hiring managers will review whatever social media and other gems they find about him on the Internet.
* Submits his resume online and then casually waits for something to happen.

Boss's Brain

* **Present:** Show that you can excel on the job today, that you will be fun to work with, that you are passionate about the company, and that you are trainable.

* **Future:** Demonstrate how you will integrate with the team and contribute to the company's growth. Show the qualities which will make you a future leader.

Chapter 2

● ● ●

Sales Strategy

Chapter Goal: Understand how deals get done from both the prospect and salesperson's point of view by mastering the concepts of the buyer's journey, sales process, and sales methodology.

*I*t's halfway through the quarter, and Alex has already exceeded *her quota. The second-strongest performer on her team is at 60 percent of quota, and no one else on her team is above 40 percent. One of her colleagues comes up and asks:*

> *"Alex, why are you so much better at pitching the product than the rest of us?"*

> *"I don't pitch the product," Alex responds.*

At this point, two other SDRs overhear the conversation and crowd around Alex's desk to learn more.

The Buyer's Journey

The first step toward mastering a sales strategy is understanding your buyer. Once you understand their pain and can address it credibly, buyers will *want* to engage with you.

While common sense might dictate that buyers know what their problem is today and want to talk to you about solving it for them, it's not that simple. As shown in figure 2.1, the buyer's journey is long and full of uncertainty.

Figure 2.1: The Buyer's Journey

As an SDR, you might enter the buyer's journey at any of the points above, and it's critical that you figure out where you are ASAP so the conversation can be as relevant and helpful as possible, and so that you can manage the process without it getting out of your control.

At any point? Even if the buyer is not aware of the problem? That's right…

Unaware of Problem: Outbound SDRs can shine here, as you plant a seed that makes buyers aware that others like them have had a problem that you have solved in the past. This is how you earn credibility!

Suspicion of Problem: Engaging at this phase allows you to help buyers define, label, and frame their suspicion. The buyer can then validate that the problem is real and begin assigning importance to its resolution.

Problem Exists: Many sellers believe that this is the ideal place to engage a prospect, but that's just plain lazy. The challenge a seller encounters when having conversations with prospects who are aware that a problem exists is that buyers have begun their process of attempting to resolve the issue. They might have started educating themselves on the subject or asking peers for their opinions. Each of these factors complicates and lengthens a sales process, and makes for challenging SDR conversations.

Explore Solutions: Here the buyer will consider your company, your competitors, a homebuilt solution, and the option to do nothing. As an SDR, your job is to get your company involved in the conversation and well-positioned against the competition.

If your messaging and interactions match buyers on their journey, you are positioned to win! In the beginning, help buyers clarify their problem. As they start to understand what they are trying to solve, you can more directly discuss how your solution might be a fit.

Think about the last time you received a prescription from your doctor. Was the script written when you walked in with symptoms, or after it was clear what problem existed and what the appropriate treatment would be?

Sales Process
In figure 2.2, we outline a sample sales process from end to end at a high level.

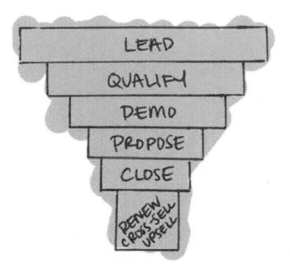

Figure 2.2: A simple sales process.

Leads are cultivated via a variety of channels, including self-sourcing, marketing, and referrals. While these prospects might be a good fit, it's not yet clear if they are, and most of the time they have not yet spoken with anyone at your company.

Qualifying involves having an initial conversation with leads, and depending on your company, the SDR and/or AE can be involved in this activity. The vendor and prospect will ask each other several questions to uncover if there is an opportunity to work together. If not, the lead is disqualified. Additional qualification involves a prospect's willingness to follow a salesperson's selling process.

Demos allow the prospect to take an in-depth look at the product. There might be several stakeholders who take part in a demo—or even several demos—led by the AE. For complex products, a sales engineer (SE) might run a demo, especially if it requires customization.

Proposals are be provided once there is a mutual commitment to do business. Ideally, they are presented in person or via webchat to the person making the buying decision.

Closing involves getting the contract signed. At this point, prospects become customers, they are invoiced, and the salesperson receives credit for the sale. Delivery of the product or service should commence shortly thereafter.

Upsells (selling more), **cross-sells** (selling a different product), and **renewals** (extending the agreement) happen over time and act as part of the extended sales process.

Sales Methodology

While the sales process includes the steps that disqualify or turn a lead into a customer, the methodology, on the other hand, prepares salespeople to navigate and maintain control of the different events that occur within that process. Methodologies do so by creating a path for salespeople to follow, replete with tactics to move selling conversations to close. Organizations that insist upon sales methodology adherence benefit from a common language, ease of evaluating individual effectiveness, a clear path toward developing professional skills, and clear coaching opportunities. These organizations are positioned to scale more effectively than those who rely on individual salespeople's "style" to move deals through the pipeline.

Popular methodologies include Sandler, MEDDIC, Solution Selling, Strategic Selling, SPIN, Challenger, and Triangle Selling.

What Does Qualified Mean?

Sales methodologies play a key role in establishing a common language around qualification. The idea is to have a standard process to qualify prospects based upon a checklist of criteria. Anyone in the company could look at any opportunity and tell you if it's qualified or not based on answers to a specific set of questions, which may include:

* Company size (relative to revenue or employees)
* Role
* Geography
* Existing products
* Job title
* Vertical market
* Specific event (funding, product launch, acquisition, government regulation)

Additional Qualification questions could focus on pain, which is covered in chapter 14.

The beauty is that everyone knows exactly what they're looking for and how to talk about it with their managers and peers. They spend less time arguing, so salespeople focus on selling and managers focus on coaching. The common language is especially helpful when looking at the handoff from the SDR to AE, which we cover in chapter 6.

Maximillian's Mishaps

* Uses the same pitch, regardless of who he is talking to and where they are on their Buyer's Journey.

* Just grinds it out, day after day, with no clarity about how he fits into his company's sales process.
* Goes with his gut in each conversation without employing a sales methodology or sales process.

Boss's Brain

* **Adherence**: Follow the process so that management has a means by which to evaluate its effectiveness. Even if it's uncomfortable at first, it's important that you fall in line.
* **Individual Growth**: Demonstrate an ability to apply the concepts of your sales methodology, which will make you a better salesperson.
* **Predictable Metrics**: Demonstrate a consistent ability to convert leads to qualified opportunities. Predictability helps ensure accurate sales forecasting, which is a top priority for sales leadership.

Chapter 3

● ● ●

The Buyer

Chapter Goal: Get to know your buyer inside out, including what they do, their pain, and how you win.

After hearing Alex talk about buyer mastery, one of her colleagues, Lazy Leonard, came over the following week, frustrated. The following exchange ensued.

Lazy Leonard: Alex, I know our buyers and their journeys, but I'm still way off pace to hit my quota.

Alex: Do you really know our buyer?

Leonard: Huh?

Alex: Think about VPs of sales. What do they do all day? And how does that change depending on the day, month, or quarter? What is their current state and what changes with our product?

Leonard: Oh...

Alex: And what pain do they experience? Not high-level fluff like "running sales reports is inefficient." What specific pain do they have that is so terrible it impacts them personally?

Leonard: Hmm...

Alex: And how have we won with sales VPs in in the past? Not companies. Specifically, what happens when someone like your prospect gives us money? How will their world change? How do they measure the benefit?

Leonard: I never thought about it that way.

Alex: Then why should they trust you?

In this chapter, we will provide a framework for learning your buyer, which is represented at a high level in figure 3.1.

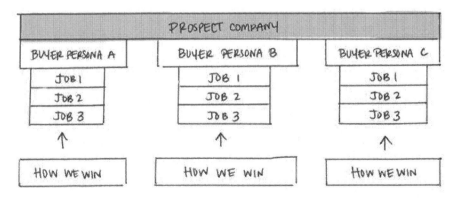

Figure 3.1: Buyer personas, their jobs, and how we win!

Buyer Personas

Imagine that your prospects have titles that include VP of sales, SVP of sales, chief revenue officer (CRO), and head of sales. While they might have slightly different duties, you are probably safe grouping all of these people together into one persona called "head of sales."

You might elaborate on this persona as follows:

The head of sales is responsible for overall revenue and profit generation. They demand results and are not interested in spending time on details. Employee professional development is important, but performance this quarter is critical. Heads of sales are tech-savvy and expect people on the team to "figure it out." They are accountable to the CEO and measured by accurate projections, growth, and strategic wins.

Having well-defined buyer personas provides a springboard for creating content and messaging that addresses and fulfills the needs and wants of your audience. Also, grouping job titles together so you have just a handful of personas keeps your efforts from becoming overly complex.

Messaging that does not resonate with buyers ends up having no impact or even negative consequences. Think about who might open e-mails with the two e-mail subject lines in figure 3.2.

Webinar: Learn 10 Salesforce admin tips to save you hours

How top sales leaders interact with their board of directors

Figure 3.2: Different strokes (subject lines) for different folks (buyer personas).

The head of sales doesn't care about salesforce admin tips, but the sales ops manager probably does. However, the head of sales definitely cares about how to interact with the board of directors!

What Do Your Buyers Do?

In order for SDRs to have professional conversations with buyers, it's critical that they understand what the buyers do all day. What are their goals, what keeps them up at night, what will cause them to earn a promotion, and what events might cause them to lose their job?

PERSONA	WHAT THEY DO
VP of MARKETING	
VP of SALES	
FINANCIAL ANALYST	
IT MANAGER	

Figure 3.3: SDRs must know their buyers.

Wait...What Do They Really Do?

A surface-level understanding of what prospects do is dangerous. You might think you know what they do, but once you begin a conversation with a real buyer, it becomes clear that you don't.

In Clayton Christensen's book *Competing Against Luck*, he talks about the concept of "Jobs to be Done" (JTBD). A job can be something complex like "making a sale," and can then be decomposed into its parts, such as "e-mailing a prospect."

Figure 3.4: Understanding what buyers do is critical.

In figure 3.4, the box on the left represents what happens before someone does a job. After that's finished, another job will be done, either by that same person or by someone else. As an SDR, you will want to know the following for each buyer persona:

* What job does your prospect perform that you can impact?
* How does that job fit into their broader set of responsibilities?
* How do they do that job today?
* What pain is associated with how they do the job today?
* Does someone important in their company care about that job being done well?
* If they don't change how they do the job, what happens?

Ideally, your product team also has a crystal-clear vision for each point above for each of your prospect personas, but if not, you have two problems:

* You also don't know this information.
* Your product was built without knowing the JTBD, so it probably won't work very well!

If you need to figure out the JTBD on your own, do your best and work at it over time, but don't use it as an excuse to avoid working toward your quota!

What Is Their Pain?

Once you know the jobs that are performed by each buyer persona from figure 3.1, next figure out which jobs involve pain that you can solve.

Salespeople know they should ask questions, but simply asking questions isn't good enough. When asking questions, make sure you are uncovering real pain and not asking for basic information that could be learned or inferred from the Internet. Otherwise, you are just going through the motions, and that is a waste of time.

It's like fishing for largemouth bass. Around dusk in the spring, the bass will be feeding around structures (logs, docks, and so on) near the shore. Casting into deep open water is a complete waste of time—there is hardly any chance fish are hanging out there. No guarantees exist that the bass will be hanging out by any given log, but since we know that bass like to hang out by logs, the chances are much better.

Asking prospects questions is similar to fishing for bass. You want to cast near the logs and boat docks, not into the middle of the lake. So let's be targeted with our prospects:

* Find pain that we can solve.
* Drill down on the pain to uncover whether it merits fixing.
* Get commitment on the urgency attributed to fixing the pain.

And if there's nothing there, disqualify and move on to the next fishing hole.

PERSONA	PAIN
VP of MARKETING	
VP of SALES	
FINANCIAL ANALYST	
IT MANAGER	

Figure 3.5: Knowing potential buyer pain points helps SDRs rapidly qualify prospects.

How Do You Win?

Unless your company is brand new or the product you sell is new to your company, you have won deals in the past. Furthermore, you have won specific types of deals with specific buyer personas before, and each of these tie to specific jobs to be done.

When a company has hundreds of customers, it doesn't make sense for every SDR to know every deal that has come in the door. Nevertheless, for each buyer persona, each SDR should have rock-solid stories to use as social proof. Imagine that you are selling a prospecting tool to the VP of sales. Which of the following resonates?

AlphaCorp bought our product, and their e-mail bounce rates fell by 5 percent.

BetaCorp was able to identify another 5,000 companies in their target market and increased revenue by 20 percent.

Both are great outcomes. Both are probably good reasons to buy your software. The VP of sales, however, likely cares a great deal more about the revenue story. By mapping the story to the buyer persona, you are not guaranteeing a win, but the probability of success will increase for sure!

PERSONA	HOW WE WIN
VP of MARKETING	
VP of SALES	
FINANCIAL ANALYST	
IT MANAGER	

Figure 3.6: SDRs must know specifically how they can win with each buyer persona.

Buyer Psychology

Buyers are conditioned to be wary of salespeople. When you walk into a store and a salesperson approaches you, chances are you quickly say, "I'm just looking…" as a means of batting back their advances. Why? Well, we all have experienced a snarky, slimy, snake-like, sleazy, slick, slippery salesperson at some point in our lives as buyers. That experience has braced us to protect ourselves from being "sold."

Instead, we initially sit back and provide as little information as possible. Then we try to get as much information as we can out of the salesperson. When that avenue is exhausted, we take to the Internet, competitors, our friends, and analysts to fill in our information gaps. We return armed with knowledge, pricing, and comparative benefits, then haggle until we get the best deal.

What we described above is a process. It's the buyer's process. We're all experts at it because we have dealt with salespeople before. Your prospects are no different. It's important that your selling system accounts for the fact that there is more noise in the marketplace than ever before. Check the inbox of the average executive—it's not uncommon to find tens of e-mail solicitations per day. Couple that with online advertising, retargeting, billboards, reports, broadcast advertising, print advertising (still)…the list goes on and on!

The bottom line is:

You must know your buyer…inside and out!

Maximillian's Mishaps

*   Thinks that prospects will schedule a meeting because he urgently needs to hit his quota.
*   Understands the buyer's journey, but hasn't a clue what the buyer's job entails and what they actually do all day long.
*   Skips over the sometimes arduous task of uncovering pain, and opts instead to list features and benefits in hopes that prospects will just "get it," or he can "generate interest."
*   Fails to understand how other deals have been won, and struggles to use previous success to influence prospects.

Boss's Brain

*   **Posture and Relevance**: Speak with prospects as if you are a peer, and do not rely on them to teach you the basics of their role.
*   **Conversions**: Use relevant messaging and customer success stories to avoid losing good leads.

Chapter 4

● ● ●

The Market

Chapter Goal: Identify the key information you should master regarding your market and competition.

*A*lex and her fellow SDRs are asked questions by their sales trainer:

> *Trainer: How do you respond when a prospect says, "Why are you better than Competitor X?"*
>
> *Feature-Loving Fran: We just came out with [Feature A], something that many of our customers have asked for, and Competitor X has publicly stated that they will not build this feature for eighteen months.*
>
> *Lazy Leonard: We just are better! Isn't that what you have read in the analyst reports?*
>
> *Alex: I don't know that we are better. Do you mind sharing a little more about your problem and why you think either our company or Competitor X might be able to help you solve it?*

The room goes silent.

Fran: There is no way they would beat us. We have Feature A!

Alex: Oh yeah? If Competitor X offered you a job paying 50 percent more money, would you decline and say, "Thanks but no thanks, I could never win a deal against Feature A?"

Ideal Customer Profile

When we are socializing with SDRs, you can always tell a "noob" fresh out of onboarding training because when we ask, "What's your ideal customer profile (ICP)," they invariably respond: "Everyone!" And we groan. Here's a recent example of the caliber of responses from an SDR team:

* **Worst Possible Answer**: Everyone
* **Terrible**: Sales teams
* **Bad**: Sales teams with Salesforce.com
* **Better**: Sales teams with 10–200 reps who use Salesforce.com
* **Good**: Sales teams with 10–200 reps who use Salesforce. com and plan on growing more than 10 percent in the next year
* **Excellent**: Sales teams with 10–200 inside sales reps who use Salesforce.com, plan on growing more than 10 percent in the next year, and the VP has previously invested in external sales consulting

The ICP might also be referred to as your "target market," and should be a well-defined segment of a broader market of people who could buy from you. If you think "everyone" is your target market, how do you segment, how do you qualify, where do you spend your energy, and how do you measure market penetration?

Verticals

Your market can be segmented into verticals to allow salespeople to specialize in certain types of deals. Verticals could be formed around an industry (health care, high tech, finance, and so on) or use case (OEM, cloud, on-premises).

While the product your company sells to each vertical is likely the same, the implementation may vary, and the messaging will be different. When salespeople specialize by vertical, they develop a more in-depth understanding of specific types of prospects. Imagine the following salespeople. Who do you think has a better understanding of the buyer?

> **Pat**: Currently selling to large and small companies in health care, financial services, high tech, nonprofit, and government.

> **Jamie**: Currently selling to large health care companies.

Jamie has the opportunity to learn the large health care space inside and out, while Pat is constantly jumping around, thereby making it hard to obtain more than a surface-level understanding of any given vertical.

Identifying Good Deals versus Bad Deals

Generally speaking, a good deal is one that, when put into a normal sales process, can close in a predictable amount of time when adhering to a predictable process. These deals are SDR gold! You know just what to say that will result in a meeting with your AE, and once the deal is passed along, the AE will accept it with a smile!

Imagine that your company sells accounting software to farmers. A good deal might be when the prospect says something like the following:

> "We have tried everything out there, but nothing fits our needs. None of the name-brand products work, and we've even attempted to build our own. We need to get something in place before our audit starts in sixty days, and our CEO has authorized us to spend whatever it takes. It would be great for you to come present to our executive team next week."

Looks pretty straightforward, right? This deal is pretty good based on what we know so far, and it should be easy to get them to take a meeting with your AE.

A bad deal, on the other hand, doesn't follow a predictable process. It absorbs significant resources and has an uncertain probability of closing with an uncertain timeline. Characteristics of a bad deal might include:

* They want to talk technical details with you before engaging with an AE.
* The prospect shows initial interest, but stops responding to e-mails and calls.
* The prospect asks for time-consuming activity or reference calls from the vendor without making any significant commitments.

As an SDR, if you know what a good deal looks like, you will know where to spend your time, and you are on your way to crushing your quota!

Industry Knowledge

Your buyers will often work in the same industry for many years, possibly their entire careers. As a result, SDRs who lack industry knowledge might find it hard to be credible when talking with prospects.

However, you might have an advantage when it comes to what is happening now. While your prospects are heads-down focused on their day jobs, you can serve as a trusted resource. Fill out figure 4.1 and highlight where your product can make an impact based on various market trends.

TREND	OPPORTUNITY	RISK
TREND A		
TREND B		
TREND C		

Figure 4.1: Stay on top of market trends.

As you work to build your knowledge around industry history and market trends, here are some things you can do:

* **Network** with people who have more industry experience and have them help fill in knowledge gaps.
* **Research** and read materials such as analyst reports and trade publications online.
* **Debrief** with AEs after they lose deals and see if there is knowledge to be learned.

The Competition

Good SDRs understand their competitors' strengths and weakness-es. Prospects often ask questions such as:

* How are you different than AlphaCorp?
* I already have BetaCorp's product. Why do I need yours?
* What makes you unique?

Without having a strong answer to these questions, it's difficult to differentiate your product in the mind of a prospect. Additionally, if you don't even know that a competitor exists, there's a good chance that prospects won't even want to speak with you because they'll think you don't know the market.

Finding Competitive Intelligence

Ideally, your company already has a standardized process of cap-turing and disseminating competitive intelligence. If not, you might want to check out the following:

* **Analyst Reports**: Gartner, Forrester, and other advisory firms analyze companies and compare their strengths and weaknesses.
* **Competitor Websites**: A lot can be learned from a compa-ny's website regarding their product, customers, and how they talk about themselves.
* **Prospects and Customers**: Prospects and customers are usually happy to tell you how you compare to other compa-nies in your space. Just ask.

Other options do exist but often blur ethical boundaries. For ex-ample, having a friend pretend to be interested in a product so you can sit in on deep-dive demos after your friend has signed an NDA is very unethical. Don't do that.

Win, Lose, and Battle

For each competitor, how do you win, how do you lose, and where is there a battle? Your company should have competitive battle cards built out similar to what is shown in figure 4.2.

HOW WE WIN	HOW WE BATTLE	HOW WE LOSE

Figure 4.2: Have a battle card for each competitor.

As an SDR, competitors should not be your main focus. If a prospect has pain you can solve, they should not eliminate you at the sales-development stage. Specific, concise, and accurate competitive talking points will help keep you in the game; then it's your AE's turn!

Digging deeper, maybe extend figure 4.2 to include the information shown in figure 4.3, where we also anticipate specific claims your competitor makes and show responses you can have handy.

This table starts to get into objection handling territory, which we cover in chapter 11.

Don't Obsess

Make sure you don't obsess over your competitors. They exist, and there's not a whole lot you can do about them. Know them. Respect them. Maybe even fear them (privately). But don't obsess.

COMPETITOR NAME	WHEN THEY CLAIM..	WE RESPOND ..
COMPETITOR X		
COMPETITOR Y		

Figure 4.3: Prepare to respond to specific statements competitors will make.

Again, as an SDR, your job is to get your company into the prospect's buying process. You will rarely need to eliminate competitors from the conversation, though you will have to demonstrate that you are in their league!

Account-Based Selling

Now that you know your buyers and your market, we can introduce the concept of account-based selling (ABS). You might hear people also refer to it as "account-based marketing" (ABM), "account-based revenue" (ABR), or "account-based sales development" (ABSD). We prefer ABS, because much like when you work on your abs at the gym, ABS requires consistent effort over time, but if you keep at it, you will see stellar results.

The idea here is that you know which accounts to target, and you can identify who your prospects are within these accounts. At that point, you begin applying the tactics you learn in this book, such as messaging, what channels to use (e-mail, phone, social media, and so on), asking for (internal) referrals, and so on. Simply put:

In an ABS model, the "prospect" is not a person, but rather an account that has many people, many of whom could be a good fit to have a conversation with your AE.

ABS is most useful when targeting enterprise prospects. Imagine that you sell to VPs of sales. If your prospect is a small company, they will only have one VP of sales, so ABS probably is not a good fit. However, large companies can have several sales VPs. As a result, you will need to plan how to reach out to all of your potential buyers across a large and complex organization, then execute. ABS will work in smaller companies as well, as long as you have several buyer personas and can strategically target them using different tactics.

Maximillian's Mishaps

* Ignores the ICP and targets any lead who will talk with him.
* Passes bad leads to AEs without communicating that they might not be a fit.
* Ignores the history of his industry relevant to the buyer and acts like his product is the most innovative thing since the wheel.
* Knows very few competitors, and readily dismisses them all as "terrible" in prospect conversations.
* Does not believe in ABS, and instead thinks if one person at a company says "no," then the entire organization is disqualified.

Boss's Brain

* **Understand the Competition:** Position your product for success against alternatives, know when to disqualify, and effectively manage a discussion about the competition.

* **Focus on Winners**: Optimize your time by spending most of it focused on the best prospects, and disqualify losers fast.
* **ABS Strategy**: Know who to target, when, with what message, and through which channels when prospecting into large accounts.

Chapter 5

● ● ●

Your Product

Chapter Goal: Learn how to talk about your product when engaging prospects. Hint: they don't care about features!

*L*azy Leonard was sipping kombucha in the lunchroom when he spotted Alex uncharacteristically staring at what looked to be a cat meme on her laptop during a break. Finally, a sign that she's human!

> **Lazy Leonard**: What's your cat's name?
>
> **Alex**: Cat? Oh—I don't have time for pets. This image is a reminder.
>
> **Leonard**: *rolling his eyes* A reminder of what?
>
> **Alex**: That our prospects don't buy the mirror. They buy the lion!

Should SDRs Talk About the Product?

Strong arguments can be made for and against having SDRs get into detailed product conversations with prospects. There is no

Figure 5.1: Prospects buy the lion...not the mirror.

clear-cut answer, and it depends on the complexity of the product, buyer expectations, and the skill level of the SDR.

Here are some arguments in favor of SDRs having product conversations:

* **Buyer Experience**: If a prospect asks to speak with you and the first question he or she asks results in a request to schedule another call...that's a bad experience.
* **Avoid Wasting AE Time**: If your AEs need to answer all product questions, they will likely spend a lot of time with unqualified buyers.
* **SDRs Should Know the Product**: The idea of working in a prospect-facing role at a company where you don't know the product is pretty silly.

There are also compelling points against having SDRs talk product:

*   **Distraction**: If you are prepping for and worried about product conversations, you are less focused on scheduling meetings and qualifying prospects.
*   **Low(er) Quality Conversation**: Even if the SDR memorizes everything, it's still tough to have an in-depth conversation with executives or technical people who have been using products like yours for more than twenty years. You will become great over time, but not in one month.
*   **Qualify First**: Experienced buyers know that SDRs are there to qualify and pass leads, so insisting on in-depth product conversations isn't something serious buyers usually do.

Product Value Proposition

What value does your product bring to your customers? Very simply:

What specifically happens when someone pays you money for your product?

In cases where that value cannot be achieved by other competitors for a similar price, that is your unique value proposition. The value proposition should lead to one or more of the following:

*   **Make Money**: Is there a compelling return on investment (ROI)?
*   **Save Money**: Can the customer directly save money?
*   **Save Time**: Time is the most precious commodity…can it be saved?
*   **Mitigate Risk**: Will the company's risk profile improve after buying your product?

There are certainly other types of value, but the weaker they are, the harder it will be to attract and retain customers. Products with unclear or poorly articulated value are difficult to sell.

Customer Success Stories

Customer success stories demonstrate the application of your value proposition to an actual customer. They can be as basic as one sentence, or as in-depth as a detailed case study. The story might include:

* **Challenge**: The problem they were trying to solve.
* **Solution**: How the product solved the problem.
* **Results**: The quantitative impact of solving the problem (more revenue, less cost, more time, and so on).

These stories can be used by various departments to accomplish their goals:

* **Marketing**: Attract leads.
* **Sales Development**: Generate enough interest to move to the sales process.
* **Account Executives**: Help prospects sell internally to executive decision-makers.
* **Customer Success**: Create a sense of urgency for user engagement.

Using these stories is an excellent example of focusing on social proof instead of product features. Talking about how others have used the product successfully is a much stronger message than talking about what buttons do when they are clicked.

The best SDRs seamlessly weave customer success stories into conversations with prospects. Imagine the two following responses to a prospect asking how the widget feature works:

> *Taylor says, "Great question! When you click on the Widget feature, four buttons pop up. If you click on the second button, the graph will change. The third button makes the colors on the graph change, which isn't that helpful..."*

> *Jamie says, "I appreciate you asking. One of our customers, Acme Corp, used the widget feature to improve accuracy by 20 percent. They were able to tie 2.1 million dollars of revenue directly to this increase in accuracy."*

Who do you think has the better pitch? Jamie, for the win!

Product Use Cases

Use cases are theoretical success stories that are not associated with a specific customer. The goal is to show prospects how using your product solves their specific problem. A success story is generally more impactful because a product use case by itself can be seen as theoretical.

You will leverage use cases when there is not a good success story for a given situation. It's not ideal, but better than nothing!

Vitamins, Candy, and Painkillers

Typically, products fit into one of these three categories. The following is an overview of how they might be distinguished:

Vitamins: Nice to have. You know they are important, but you can live without them. An example is cell phone replacement insurance.

Candy: Create pleasure. These are products that promote a benefit, but again, you can live without them. Examples include season tickets for sporting events and country club memberships.

Painkillers: Solve pain. If you live without these products, you will still be in pain. Examples include accounting software or CRMs.

Here are a few tips to avoid making your painkiller sound like a vitamin or candy:

* Identify the prospect's specific pain.
* Ensure the prospect understands exactly how your product solves their pain.
* Whenever they say something is "cool" or "neat," ensure it's because it solves their critical pain points, not just because they think it's flashy.

If the prospect still doesn't see how your product is a painkiller and you think it is, use their specific objections and ask if you can schedule a call with your AE to dig a little deeper. If they have pain, they should take the call!

Product Demos

While AEs typically perform demos, here is a short section here to give you a peek into your future duties.

Demos are where you show prospects how a product works, and they can vary in length from a few minutes to an hour or more. Sometimes a short slide deck is presented before a demo to set the stage, but realize that most people hate sitting through slide presentations. As an SDR, make sure you set the stage for what will happen during the demo so there are no surprises.

With most products, prospects want to see what they can do before making a purchase decision. During a demo, the prospect will be focused on a few key areas:

* Does the product do what the sales rep says it does?
* Can it solve my problem?
* How hard is it to use?
* What doesn't it do that I might need to solve my problem?
* Does it fit all of my requirements (security, access, and so on)?
* How does it compare to competing products?

Satisfying these questions and anything else that may come up builds a level of comfort with the product and moves the prospect one step closer to a purchase decision. If the prospect wants to cover anything specific in the demo, make sure you let your AE know so he or she can prepare.

Remember that prospects don't care about specific features; they care about solving their pain. Sure, the features help solve their pain, but instead of sequentially going through the product's capabilities in a predetermined order, great presenters tell stories that resonate with the prospect.

If the prospect has a specific pain that can be solved by the product, walk them through exactly how the product solves the pain. A strong demo:

* Highlights how the product can be used in a way relevant to the prospect.
* Focuses on customer success stories.
* Avoids regurgitating features and benefits.
* Allows the prospect to ask questions and guide the direction of the demo along specific areas of interest.
* Avoids buzzwords that will distract from the core demo experience.

Sometimes it will become apparent mid-demo that the product is not a fit for the prospect (at least at this time). Signs that a demo is going poorly include:

* **Silence**: People aren't asking questions or talking much at all.
* **Hostility**: There is constant doubt or complaints regarding your product or company.
* **Apathy**: No one seems that excited about what they're seeing.

If it sounds like the demo is not resonating or the prospects might no longer be interested, it's a good idea to:

* Pause the demo
* Ask some open-ended questions to see how they feel
* Shift directions before you proceed

Maybe they were just confused and the questions clarified this confusion. However, they might realize they either don't have a need or the resources to implement your solution. In cases like these, it might make sense to walk away from the deal and focus time on higher-value prospects.

Product Release Notes

If you are expected to talk product with prospects, make sure you frequently review release notes, which are summaries of changes to the product. These notes highlight new features and their impact on the user experience, as well as known bugs and issues that might affect a user's ability to use the product.

There are typically two types of release notes:

Engineering: Detail the changes from a technical perspective. While detailed and helpful, they are not easily understood by a nontechnical audience.

Customer: Focused on the changes that impact how customers use the product. For example, if there are new screens, buttons, or other features, they should be highlighted. They will also cover fixes to any known issues and report new known bugs.

If your prospects use a free trial before or while you're engaged with them, it's critical that you know what's going on with the product. Imagine how bad your company would look if prospects know more than the sales team about recent product changes!

Another use of release notes is to follow up with old leads that never converted but expressed interest in features that have since been built. Imagine the two ways we could follow up with a lead we haven't talked to in a while:

Good: When we spoke four months ago, you expressed interest in Feature X. I wanted to let you know that we took your input seriously and it's now in the product. Let me know if you'd like to catch up next week.

Bad: I'm checking in to see if you'd like to have another conversation about [Your Company Name].

See what happened here? Play chess, not checkers.

Maximillian's Mishaps

* Thinks that talking about product features and benefits is selling.
* Does not use customer stories when talking about his product.
* Fails stay current with product release notes and messaging.

Boss's Brain

* **Storytelling**: Learn to tell specific stories about how your product solved someone else's problem. Prospects don't care about your features.
* **Scheduled Meetings**: Find pain that the product can solve, then define the value of scheduling a meeting with the AE.

Chapter 6

• • •

Working with Account Executives

Chapter Goal: Develop ideas to help you and your AEs ensure one another's mutual success.

*A*lex was recently at a happy hour with her fellow SDRs when the topic of working with AEs came up.

Lazy Leonard: I don't think my AE likes me.

Feature-Loving Fran: I'm certain mine hates me!

Leonard: What the heck am I supposed to do? I'm trying everything, and I have no idea how to make this work. Alex, you got lucky...you got a good match.

Alex shakes her head in disgust, pulls out her laptop, and proceeds to open up three e-mails from when she started, showing her AE's harsh criticism of her discovery notes.

Alex: Instead of complaining, I asked for some feedback.

Keep Them Busy!

There are two things that the best AEs do:

1. Spend most of their time meeting with prospects who have a good chance of closing, while minimizing time spent on losers or admin tasks.
2. During the meetings, they execute their playbooks.

You can't control #2, but how the AEs spend their day is up to you! Look at figure 6.1 and tell me that Rep B has any chance of outperforming Rep A...even if he or she is a much better salesperson.

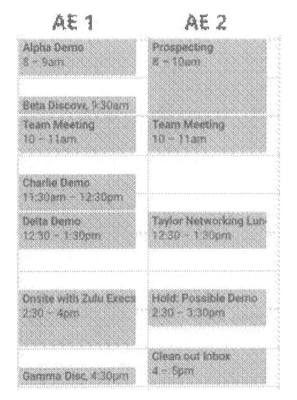

Figure 6.1: Who has better chance of hitting their quota?

Successful SDRs will keep their AEs' calendars *full* of *quality* meetings!

Start Ahead...Or At Least Neutral

Prospects should have a positive (or at least neutral) view of your company the first time they speak with an AE. Winning against the competition is tough. It's much harder when you are coming from behind.

Reasons that prospects would have a negative view of your company include:

* **Scheduling Snafus**: Did they get the wrong calendar invite, or was it sent multiple times?
* *Groundhog Day* (**Bill Murray movie**): Is the AE asking the same questions you asked, making prospects feel like they are living the same thing over and over again?
* **Mixed Messaging**: Do marketing, sales development, and AEs all talk about the product the same way, or is the prospect confused because everyone is saying something different?
* **Free-Trial Experience**: Did they have trouble using the free trial (if you have one)?

The first three points are controlled by the SDR. As for the fourth, you should be able to get them back on track before passing them along to an AE. Maybe coach them on the trial or offer some other insight into how the product would work for them. Passing along a frustrated prospect is probably a waste of every-one's time.

SDR-to-AE Hand-Off Process

Imagine that you're back in school and you just wrote a great paper. The best one you've ever written. You know it's a shoo-in to get an A+...but you forget to turn it in. As a result, you get a zero and lose credibility with your professor.

That's exactly what happens when the SDR-to-AE hand-off process doesn't go well. You will lose the prospect, and the AE will not be in your fan club.

Some tips for a great handoff include:

* **Efficiency**: Make it easy! Don't turn this process into a science project for the prospect or the AE.
* **Standardized Notes**: The AE should be able to scan your notes and get the point. Not too much. Not too little. The structure should also be the same for every opportunity you pass.
* **Confidence**: Show the prospect that your company knows what it's doing! If you can't transition from the SDR to AE, can you build a reliable product?

During the handoff, you should be on the phone to kick off the call by introducing the prospect to the AE. It sounds simple, but the prospect is likely still skeptical of committing to doing business with you, so a strong introduction can help improve confidence. Consider the following examples:

Good: [Prospect Name], I'd like to introduce you to [AE Name], who is an account executive on our team and will be working with you moving forward. We have debriefed on our prior conversation(s), so you won't have to repeat yourself.

[AE Name] has great expertise in working with CEOs in start-up organizations—like you. I'll let you two take it from here.

Bad: [Prospect Name], meet [AE Name]. [AE Name], meet [Prospect Name]. OK, I'll hop off here.

See the difference here? The former is professional and instills confidence. The latter could make someone question the strength of your organization.

Also, while it's fine to talk, e-mail, and chat with your AE, if the information is not in the CRM, it doesn't exist. Be vigilant to ensure that all real deals are updated so your teammates have what they need to be successful once they accept your handoff.

SDR-to-AE Information Transfer

When AEs read your notes, they should be able to pick up from there and move the deal forward. Everything you were supposed to ask should be covered, and if anything was skipped, a note should be made. The AE should look at the deal in the CRM and think, "Wow! I'm excited about this opportunity!"

The biggest information-transfer mistakes SDRs make are around:

*   **Missing Information**: If you are supposed to ask about budget, but you didn't ask about budget...what are you doing?
*   **Excess Information**: Be concise and limit the notes to important information.
*   **Formatting**: The notes should be easy to read and use only common language (don't make up your own abbreviations).

It's fine to take rough notes in the moment, but clean them up before passing them along. Even if you think they're great, our advice is to aggressively seek feedback on your notes by doing something like the following:

*   Talk to an AE (in person) and say, "I'm trying to get better at taking notes while talking with prospects. Would you mind giving me honest critical feedback on how I can get better?"
*   Take his or her advice to heart, even if you disagree.
*   Repeat this process with multiple AEs.
*   Share your progress over time as you improve.

The last point is critical! People love seeing the fruits of their labor, and if they feel like their advice had an impact, they will be more willing to offer their thoughts in the future.

Securing In-Person Meetings for Your AE

It's challenging to get a prospect to reply to your e-mails or calls, but it's much harder to secure an in-person meeting. Maybe your AEs never meet prospects in person, but if they do, here are some tips:

*   **Have an Offer**: Why would prospects want to meet with you in person? Do you have a diagram to review? Would a whiteboarding session help them clarify and start the path toward solving a problem? The prospects must feel like they will learn something valuable as a result of the meeting.
*   **Develop an Agenda**: Ensure that there is a tight agenda and that the prospects can add items they want to cover. The agenda helps justify the time commitment and demonstrates that you are there for business and not a casual discussion.

* **Confirm the Attendees**: If your prospect is the CIO and extends an invitation to his or her IT director, then the CIO decides not to attend, the meeting will likely not achieve its desired result. Ensure the right people are at the meeting or reschedule.

You will usually only get one chance for an in-person meeting. If your product is not a hit with the most powerful people in the room, the sales process will likely end, and you won't be invited back.

Make Sure Prospects Show Up

If a prospect doesn't show, you will not get paid, and the AE will be frustrated. Not a good situation. Your job is to schedule meetings *and* make sure everyone shows up.

Here are a few tactics to ensure that prospects show up for meetings:

* When scheduling, ask if there is any reason they might not be able to attend.
* In the invite, ask them to let you know if anything comes up that could cause them to reschedule.
* E-mail an hour before the meeting, confirming that it's still on.

People have different opinions on the last point. Some say that "confirming a meeting" is explicitly giving a prospect an opportunity to cancel. If your confirmations frequently result in cancellations, skip this step and see if anything changes.

If they still don't show, here are some ideas for a meeting that was scheduled for 10:00:

* **10:03**: E-mail the prospect, asking if he or she is still able to attend.
* **10:06**: Call the prospect. Leave a voicemail if there is no answer.
* **10:10**: Call one more time. If there is no answer, leave a voicemail saying that you will reschedule.
* **10:11**: Send an e-mail to reschedule.

Use your emotional intelligence to weigh the trade-offs between being persistent and annoying. If they show up and hate you because you bugged them too much, that's not good either. Keep in mind that if you scheduled a meeting, that means that you uncovered pain. You are not pestering prospects, but instead you are endeavoring to work on their behalf to resolve a problem that they have shared with you.

Do you see how failing to uncover pain puts you in poor position?

SDR–AE One-on-Ones

SDRs should have periodic one-on-one meetings with their AEs to talk about the account-planning strategy and how things are going in general. During these meetings, they can go over status updates, any roadblocks that have popped up, and share success stories.

There should be an agenda prepared in advance that both parties can edit. A meeting without an agenda is a discussion, and discussions don't accomplish much. Any relevant topics, including the current deals in the SDR's pipeline, should be discussed during this meeting.

The following examples describe meetings with different levels of preparedness:

No One Prepares: The AE and SDR pick a couple of random topics to discuss and maybe do a surface-level pipeline review. Not much gets accomplished.

One Person Prepares: The other person isn't prepared, so conversation gets bumped to the next meeting. The person who prepared is frustrated that he or she invested time for no reason.

Both People Prepare: Each person contributes productively, and even if topics need to be bumped to the next meeting, they do the best they can this week.

Maximillian's Mishaps

* Works in a silo without regard to sales team directives or AE goals.
* Trusts prospects when they willingly schedule a meeting, and is surprised when they don't show up.
* Neglects to put information in the CRM before handing off leads his AE. Instead, he takes rough notes and forces the AE to figure it out.
* Lacks pre-call preparation and therefore fumbles handoffs to the AE.
* Lacks urgency to keep his AE's calendar full.

Boss's Brain

* **Relationships:** Whether in a round robin or paired system, develop productive and performing relationships with AEs.

No one wants to manage a prima donna, arbitrate petty arguments, or endure finger-pointing.

* **Consistency:** Produce results. Consistently. Wild vacillations in activity, productivity, or results demonstrate immaturity in the role.
* **Held Meetings:** Hold prospects accountable to their commitments, and anticipate flakiness. When prospects fail to show for a meeting, it is costly and leads to missed goals.

Chapter 7

• • •

E-mail

Chapter Goal: Master e-mail subject lines, bodies, signatures, and maybe even become inspired to start using video as part of your e-mail strategy.

*W*hen Alex started working as an SDR, she struggled to get people to respond to her e-mails. Heck, she was lucky if people even opened them! Then one day, she realized something she had been missing:

> Success with prospecting e-mails is bigger than just mastering concepts around e-mail. It's about using e-mail as a tool to apply what is known about the buyer and then scaling these efforts once success is found.

It's with this realization that Alex started to piece together one of the keys to success that takes many people years and that some are never able to grasp:

> Sales isn't about learning one skill and moving to the next. It's about mastering all of the independent skills and then evolving how they are used together.

The Subject Line (a.k.a. "The Bait")

When you go fishing, the point of the bait is to tell the fish:

Hey fishy! Come over here. Nibble on this thing. Doesn't it look delicious?

Subject lines are very similar. Just substitute a few words, and you have:

Hey prospect! Look at this e-mail! Doesn't the subject line look so compelling that you want to open it up and see what's inside?

Strong subject lines encourage the receiving party to open the e-mail, check out its contents, and potentially respond to the call to action (CTA).

The problem is that your fish are overwhelmed with the amount of bait in the water, and they are not hungry. How can you stand out?

What Is a Good Subject Line?

The best lines are:

* **Short**: The preview text will be readable in their inbox without opening the e-mail.
* **Relevant**: The reader can tell what the e-mail is about by looking at the subject line.
* **Not Misleading**: Tricking people might get you good open rates, but bad follow-through.

Want some examples? Let's start with a few subject lines Maximillian is fond of:

"**Checking In**": Terrible. Checking in about what? You have no value to offer the reader.

"**Expand your reach with social media**": Too vague. Looks like a generic sales e-mail.

"**Introducing Acme Pro**": What? I don't know what this is. Oh! It's a product pitch! Duh!

Before we get to the good ones, here are a few more from Maximillian:

"**Learn how [Company Name] created [Description of Your Product] to solve

[Problem You Solve] for [Name of Customer]**": Way too long! Come on!

"**YOU HAVE TO SEE THIS E-MAIL**": Don't yell. It's rude. And why do I have to see it?

"**Re: Free Pizza Thursday**": Don't misrepresent the nature of the e-mail, unless you really are sending free pizza, and it's "Re:" because you are responding to something they sent you!

"**Are you open to meting with me Thrusday?**": Spelling errors are deadly.

OK, now that you know what not to do, here are some better examples:

"Ten Minutes to Discuss [Problem You Solve]?": If they have that problem, they will probably open it.

"How [Customer Name] Solved [Problem You Solve]": Again, if they have the problem, they might take a look.

"[Topic Related to Your Product] Event in [Prospect City]": If relevant, they might want to come!

"Referral from [Person Prospect Knows]": If this person *actually* gave a referral, there is a compelling reason to open the e-mail.

"[Prospect Name]—[Topic They Care About] Report for You!": Using their name can be intriguing.

Obviously, you need to fill in the brackets based on what makes sense for your company, but hopefully you are getting some ideas.

What Are Good Open Rates?

E-mail open rates are a vanity metric that doesn't directly lead to a positive outcome, such as the creation of an opportunity or revenue. Yes, people need to open your e-mail, but if SDR A has a 20 percent open rate and SDR B has a 40 percent open rate, that tells us nothing important. Plus, the fact that someone had an X percent open rate last year doesn't tell you anything about what it should be the following year.

One thing you might do is form a hypothesis that states:

If I can get open rates to increase from X percent to Y percent, then that should create Z more opportunities for my AE.

If you can do that, you're golden!

The Body of the E-mail

Now that someone has opened your e-mail (congrats on that great subject line!), the next step is to convince them to respond to your call to action (CTA). Most likely, the CTA is a request to do one of the following:

* Respond to the e-mail
* Click on a link and visit a website

Here are a few overarching principles to consider when thinking about e-mail bodies:

* **Be Concise**: Use the fewest number of words possible while still making the point.
* **Easily Scannable**: The recipient should be able to get the point without focusing too hard.
* **Stand-Alone**: Don't reference other e-mails that your prospect likely didn't read or doesn't remember. You know your e-mail sequence. They don't!
* **Relevance**: WIIFM—What's In It for Me? Irrelevance will lead to a quick delete!

A quick point on relevance. Relevance *does not* mean personalized. If you spend time making a custom e-mail for each individual prospect, you will *never* hit your number. Instead of creating a science project, make a spreadsheet that looks something like figure 7.1. You can also keep this information in your e-mail cadence tool if you have the ability to easily organize e-mails.

PERSONA	EMAIL #	POINT TO MAKE	CTA	EMAIL COPY
PERSONA A	1	POINT 1	CTA 1	
	2	POINT 2	CTA 2	
	3	POINT 3	CTA 3	
PERSONA B	1	POINT 4	CTA 4	
	2	POINT 5	CTA 5	
	3	POINT 6	CTA 6	

Figure 7.1: An index of targeted e-mails.

Here you can create relevant e-mail copy for each persona while maintaining an index of e-mails in one place. Also consider including columns to hold the subject line, industry vertical, and other ways you want to segment your messages. Ideally, this exercise is done collaboratively with your team so the burden does not fall completely on your shoulders.

Let's take a look at some good and bad examples of e-mail bodies. Since we want to end on a high note, we will start with the bad.

Maximillian's E-mail Examples
These are all real e-mails we have received from fairly well-known companies, and they are exactly the type of messages Maximillian would send. While we are not calling out the offenders specifically,

we use real e-mails to keep this section from being an academic exercise.

This one is terrible, yet so many people use a similar variation:

> *Just in case you missed it, bubbling this to the top of your inbox...*
>
> *[Signature]*

These types of e-mails are garbage and indicate to the prospect that you only have one thing to say of value (the first e-mail) and expect them to enter a sales process as a result. Good luck!

Here's one where, instead of *"I sent you an e-mail and have nothing valuable to add,"* the SDR essentially says, *"You read something on our site and I have nothing valuable to add."*

> *A while ago, you viewed our guide, [Name of Guide]. I wanted to make sure you didn't have any outstanding questions.*
>
> *Can I assist you by setting up a call for you to learn more?*
>
> *[Signature]*

Then, the following comes a few days later from the same person:

> *[Prospect Name],*
>
> *I am checking in on the e-mails that I have sent you to see if we could answer any questions you might have about our guide that you viewed.*

Are you interested in learning more?

[Signature]

Apparently, the recipient took the time to download a guide and possibly read it, but instead of building on the value of the guide, the e-mails shout, *"I need to hit my meeting- set quota! Help me!"* Your prospects don't care about your quota.

OK, one more then we'll move on to the good stuff. This one comes toward the end of a self-service free trial of a software product:

I wanted to get in contact with you before you [Product Name] trial end.s How do you feel about [Product Name] so far?

Reaching out to see if we can hop on a call to discuss our different plans. What day can we discuss your next steps?

Is that English? No, those aren't typos in this book. And yes, that's "you" instead of "your." And we didn't accidentally leave out the [Prospect Name] or [Signature] here…the SDR did that for us! Are you kidding?

Oh, and any e-mail that is super-long or uses buzzwords is bad, but we figured we didn't need a whole page to get that point across!

Good E-mail Examples

Now for the "magic bullet" e-mail that will get you a meeting with anyone!

Oh, we have some bad news. There isn't one. Even if we put the best e-mail templates in the world in this chapter, here's what would happen:

1. All SDRs would use them;
2. prospects would get used to them;
3. they would stop working.

We will give some general examples, but be creative and build what works for you based on the principles we set forth earlier (concise, scannable, stand-alone, and relevant). Let's expand on these principles a little more, starting with the very abstract figure 7.2.

Figure 7.2: Scannable e-mails will convert at a higher rate.

You don't know what it says, but that sure looks like an easy-to-read e-mail, eh? It nails the principles of being concise and scannable.

As for stand-alone, the reader should be able to scan through the e-mail and understand:

* Why you're reaching out
* What you want
* Why it would make sense to give you want you want

If not, rewrite it! Maybe your result will look something like this one:

[Prospect Name],

We work with [Prospect Persona]s to solve [Pain 1], [Pain 2], and [Pain 3]. In fact, we recently helped [Relevant Company] produce [Credible Result].

Would you be open to a quick call to explore a mutual fit?

If so, let me know a couple of times that work this week.

[Signature]

Boom! It's not rocket science. Remember those two e-mails we showed in the "bad" section dealing with the "guide" someone downloaded? What if, instead, the SDR wrote:

[Prospect Name],

I noticed you recently downloaded [Document Name]. After reading this document [Prospect Persona]s like yourself sometimes realize that they need help with [Problem You Solve].

Did you have this reaction as well? Our company has helped the [Prospect Persona] at companies like [Relevant Customer 1] and [Relevant Customer 2] solve this same problem.

If you'd like to chat, please let me know a couple of options that work.

[Signature]

See what we did there? Concise. Scannable. Stand-alone. Relevant. Boom!

What about the trial follow-up we saw in the bad examples? If you have a free trial as part of your sales process, our recommendation is to have three types of follow-up messaging, depending on the prospect's engagement during the trial:

> **No Engagement**: Acknowledge they are busy and set up a call.

> **Moderate Engagement**: Understand why they didn't engage more. Did they get what they need out of the product, or did they hit a wall and give up?

> **High Engagement**: Reinforce the value and close!

See why keeping an index of your e-mails is important? Writing each combination on the fly is a terrible waste of time and prone to error.

E-mail Signature

E-mail signatures do two things:

> **Reinforce Credibility**: A good signature shows you work for a real company, are not scared to provide your contact details, and that you understand professional formatting.

> **Promote Something**: If you have an upcoming event, new product video, or even an interesting book to read, you can promote this information in your signature.

While there are many variations of good signatures, here is a minimalist version that we like:

Full Name
Title | Company
Phone | E-mail
Link to Something You Are Promoting

Keep it simple. There is no reason to use monster font, large images, or inspirational quotes.

E-mail Sequences

Since most e-mail open rates are well below 100 percent, it makes sense to enroll prospects in e-mail sequences, which means they will receive a series of messages over time and will stop receiving these when certain actions are triggered.

In reality, you will also include calls, social touches, and hopefully something creative like direct mail in your sequences. Here's an example:

* **Day 1**: E-mail sent—no response
* **Day 2**: Call—no answer
* **Day 3**: Send a copy of *The Sales Enablement Playbook* via direct mail
* **Day 4**: E-mail sent—no response
* **Day 5**: Comment on LinkedIn post
* **Day 8**: E-mail sent—response—end of sequence!

Sequences should be "professionally persistent": frequent enough to drive to a goal, but not annoying. A good rule of thumb is that a prospect should be touched in each channel every three to six days.

Tags

If you have an e-mail sequence tool, you can likely insert tags, which are variables that pull values from your CRM. You have seen examples these already in this chapter...things like [Persona A], [Signature], and [Prospect Name].

If you use these tags intelligently *and* you have clean data, they can amplify the relevance of e-mails. However, if you overuse them or your data isn't clean, your e-mail will be full of typos and inaccurate information.

The key is to make sure you proofread a handful of sample e-mails using the tags, and if anything looks fishy, revisit the e-mail before approving the sequence.

Break-up Messages

Break-up messages are used at the end of a sequence when "positive" communication has not been effective with a prospect. Instead of declaring a lead lost after no response or no clear next steps, one last attempt can be made with a break-up message.

The idea here is to send a "negative" message that will trigger an emotional response. If prospects have just been putting you off and waiting for the right time, then this message could get them to make their move. If someone is not serious at all, then you will know where you stand and will be able to move on to other leads.

An example of a break-up message could be:

> *"Pat, it looks like you are no longer interested in evaluating ExampleCorp. If I'm correct, please let me know, and I will close your file."*

Any response in this scenario is a win because it accomplishes your goal of understanding where the deal stands. While break-up messages are "negative," they can still be highly professional.

A successful break-up message earns a response from the prospect. Maybe they say:

> *"Sorry, I've been slammed. Can we talk in three weeks? Ping me then. I'm still interested."*

A/B Testing

A great way to make sure you get the most out of e-mail is to run A/B tests. The idea is that you use Message A on a small group of people, use Message B on another small group, and whichever message resonates the most is then sent to the rest of your list.

A/B tests can be run on subject lines, e-mail copy, CTAs...heck, pretty much anything associated with your e-mails! Don't make testing a distracting science project, but if you're toying around with new ideas, it might be a good option instead of putting all your eggs in one basket.

Then, once you find what works, stick with it!

Using Video

Why would anyone want to read an e-mail when they can watch an e-mail? Instead of just writing text to your prospect, change it up from time to time and send a video. Done right, video e-mails are incredibly engaging and allow you to deliver a multidimensional message.

One of our favorite things to do is record a video in the corner of the screen while working through a document with the rest of the screen. You are now able to supplement your words with body language and a step-by-step walk-through of the point you are trying to make. This method can be much better than writing text while trying to describe the contents of an attachment or external website.

But *please!* Leave your fraternity and sorority clothes at home on "prospect-video-shoot" day. Just because you work at a tech company with a casual dress code doesn't mean you should wear the same outfit you wear to boozy brunch with your friends on Sundays.

Don't Send *Spam!*

Spam is nonconsensual e-mail. Don't send spam, ever. Believe it or not, it's actually illegal. E-mail was so heavily used (and abused) as an outlet that in 2003, the FTC introduced CAN-SPAM (Controlling the Assault of Non-Solicited Pornography And Marketing) to discourage and limit the use of unwarranted e-mail as a means of selling to strangers.

Sending spam not only turns off prospective customers, but hurts both your reputation and that of your company. When someone receives spam, you decrease their likelihood of ever talking to you, even if they may be interested in your product. Best case, they ignore you. They can also report messages as spam, which will hurt your domain name's credibility and reduce future deliverability rates of e-mails.

In the long run, it's better to invest effort into building a deeper connection: send white papers, data sheets, or other types of information that can help add value to your prospect.

Also, if someone asks to unsubscribe from your list, you should unsubscribe them from your list. Don't argue about it.

Marketing–Sales Messaging Alignment

While you probably have lots of flexibility around what you say in e-mail, it's important to ensure that your company's messaging stays consistent. Imagine the following:

* Marketing says you do A, B, and C
* Sales development says you do B, D, and E
* AEs focus on A, C, and D

If this pattern emerges, how do you think your prospects feel? They will think you're crazy...and you will probably scare them off!

While creativity is good, make sure anything you say to prospects does not distract from the company's general message. Even if you are able to get a couple of meetings scheduled in the short term by being aggressive with messaging, word will get out that your company is all over the place, and it will hurt your ability to hit your future goals.

Maximillian's Mishaps

* Uses long, confusing, and misleading email subject lines.
* Emails novels or short, casual, and confusing blurbs.
* Makes up his own messaging that conflicts with marketing.
* Wears inappropriate clothing in prospecting videos.

Boss's Brain

* **Quality**: Any executive in your company should be able to stand behind the emails you send. Think through your sequences from the perspective of the buyer and be aware of timing.
* **Results**: Continue to calibrate your email activity until the use of email leads to the expected number of sales opportunities created. Then, don't take your eye off of the metrics—changes can happen quickly.
* **Alignment**: Ensure that your email efforts align with the messaging and cadence goals of the marketing team, as well as the AEs you support.

Chapter 8

• • •

Phone

Chapter Goal: Improve your phone skills by learning some simple tricks, becoming resilient, and improving your buyer empathy.

*A*lex and her colleagues were at lunch one day talking about pros-pecting, and the following conversation ensued:*

Lazy Leonard: Cold calling doesn't seem to be working for me anymore.

Feature-Loving Fran: How many dials did you make yesterday?

Leonard: I think twenty or so. Maybe only fifteen, but I was preoccupied.

Fran: Step it up. I make seventy a day, but my results are pretty bad too. I get in these deep conversations about product features, but then the prospect doesn't want to talk with my AE.

Alex: Cold calling is working for me. Maybe you are all doing it wrong!

Alex's insight is spot-on. Just because something doesn't work for Person A doesn't mean that it doesn't work. Before discounting any medium, especially one as important as the phone, it's wise to ensure best efforts have been made and people are not dismissing a tool because they use it wrong. In this case, Leonard isn't putting in the effort, and Fran is talking about features instead of uncovering pain.

To Script or Not to Script? That is the Question...

Most people hate scripts. We get that. For the sake of argument, assume that "script" in this context refers to a set of points to be made, and don't need to be spoken word-for-word.

DON'T—SOUND—LIKE—A—R-O-B-O-T!

The script should sound natural, and the prospect should feel like they are talking with a real businessperson. You also should sound confident when going off script. Prospects can pick up on nervousness or confusion, which is bad.

The beginning of the script will vary based on if the lead reached out to you (inbound) or if you are reaching out cold (outbound). Let's explore the differences.

Opening Calls with Inbound Prospects

The inbound lead reached out to you, or at least filled out a web form, so your conversation has a starting point. Your CRM should show exactly what action the person has taken, including documents downloaded, events attended, e-mails opened, and so on, and this activity can be the starting point of your conversation. You should also have access to their persona, market segment, and other relevant factors.

Before picking up the phone, think for a minute, anticipate where the conversation might go, and have your social proof ready. Remember in chapter 3 where we talked about the importance of knowing your buyer and providing relevant social proof? Well, here is a specific point in the selling process where that becomes valuable.

If your inbound lead is a CFO and has downloaded White Paper 1, then you can hypothesize that he or she has Pain A, which is solved by Feature X. How do you talk about how you can help? *Not* by describing how Feature X works…but rather by talking about how Feature X solved the pain in the context of Case Study 2 and Customer Story 3, as shown in figure 8.1.

PERSONA	PAIN	FEATURE	CONTENT
CFO	PAIN A	FEATURE X	WHITEPAPER 1 CASE STUDY 2 CUSTOMER STORY 3

Figure 8.1: The "Bray–Sorey Matrix" that shows how content should tie to features, pain, and personas.

We are *not* suggesting that you call your lead (the CFO) and just start talking about Case Study 2 and Customer Story 3. However, when you start the conversation, these are the most powerful tools you have at your disposal, so know them well and be able to reference them in conversation. Beware, your hypothesis might be wrong, so be ready to pivot the conversation to additional pain points relevant to this persona.

Unfortunately, there is no perfect way to open a call. You are dealing with people, so what resonates with one individual might not work for another. Let's take a look at a few ways calls can be opened, along with commentary on why these methods may or may not be a good idea.

Imagine that your prospect is the CFO in the example above, their name is Pat, and you are Taylor Smith, an SDR at Alpha Corp.

> *Example 1: Pat, this is Taylor Smith from Alpha Corp. You recently expressed interest in our company, so I wanted to check in and see if you have any questions.*

Does Pat consider downloading a white paper "expressing interest?" If not, you might have already spooked your prospect. Avoid using the "expressed interested" phrase unless the prospect sends a note saying, "I want to talk to you."

Also, "see if you have any questions" is *soooo weak*. With this statement, you are essentially asking your prospect to become the salesperson because you have nothing interesting to discuss. What about this one?

> *Example 2: Pat, this is Taylor Smith from Alpha Corp. I'm calling because you recently downloaded a white paper from our site.*

Pat is a busy executive and there's a good chance that your white paper is not top of mind. A prospect's initial reaction to an opener like this one can be, "I don't know what you're talking about. Oh...yeah... I kind of remember..." Is that how you want to start the conversation?

Example 3: Pat, this is Taylor Smith from Alpha Corp. Have you had a chance to read White Paper 1?

Now you are being specific and opening up the opportunity to either discuss what Pat thought, or if it has not been read yet, provide a quick summary. As you learn what the prospect found interesting, you can now tie in social proof from Case Study 2 and Customer Story 3, which will drive toward setting a meeting.

Example 4: Pat, this is Taylor from Alpha Corp. Do you have two minutes?

You will learn a lot from their reaction here, including:

* Does the prospect recognize Alpha Corp?
* Is he or she excited or frustrated that you called?
* Will the prospect talk for two minutes, brush you off, or explicitly say "don't call me anymore?"

Also, be ready for the "about what?" response, since they might not know who you are.

Example 5: Pat, it's Taylor from Alpha Corp.

That's it. Stop right there. As in the example above, you can learn a lot based on their reaction.

Opening Calls with Outbound Prospects

The dreaded cold call.

Let's first examine the cold call from the buyer's perspective, using Pat the CFO from the previous section. If you don't understand this part, you will be banging your head against the wall for the next couple of months.

The Buyer's Point of View

It's Tuesday, October 2. Yesterday was the first day of the fourth quarter, so Pat's team is hard at work closing the books and preparing Q3 financial reports. They are behind on their annual goals, so the CEO needs last quarter's results ASAP. Here is how Pat's day starts:

* 6–7:00 a.m.: Wake up and get dressed.
* 7–8:00: Get kids off to school.
* 8–8:30: Commute to work.
* 8:30: Arrive at office, deal with e-mails.
* 8:39: Computer freezes. Restart. GRRRRR…
* 8:46: It's a PC, so we're now back online.
* 9:00: Exec team meeting.
* 9:30: Finance team meeting.
* 10:00: Call with auditors to prepare preaudit.
* 10:20: An analyst found a problem that required Pat to dive in.
* 10:40: Pat preps for 11:00 meeting with the team.
* 10:43: Phone rings. It's you.

Put yourself in Pat's shoes for a minute. The CEO is demanding a quick turnaround on the month-end financials, the day has been filled with nonstop action since the crack of dawn, and here you are trying to put Pat into a sales process that will add several meetings to an already impossible calendar. Ask yourself:

What on earth can you say to Pat at 10:43 a.m. on Tuesday, October 2 to add one more thing to the to-do list?

The Seller's Point of View

It's Tuesday, October 2 and the second day of a new quarter! Three more months to crush quota. The plan is to make seventy calls and send about one hundred e-mails per day.

A new list of CFOs just came in from marketing, and it's time to get started. If one says no, that's cool...just move on to the next. The comp plan is heavily weighted toward scheduling meetings with AEs, so that's the only focus.

*   8:00 a.m.: Start making calls.
*   8:23: First connect. Ten-minute conversation, but too small.
*   8:45: Second connect. Five-minute conversation. Perfect fit. Passed to AE.
*   9:15–9:30: Break.
*   9:30: More calls.
*   10:30: Wow...no one wants to talk. Keep pushing!
*   10:43: Pat, this is Taylor Smith with Alpha Corp...

Opening Calls to Create Buyer–Seller Alignment

It's 10:43 a.m. and Pat is already prepping for an 11:00 a.m. meeting. How much time do you think you can get? The physical maximum is seventeen minutes, but if you can get any time at all, one to three minutes is more realistic.

During this short period, can you identify the following?

* Pat has a problem that you can solve.
* This problem is important to Pat...ideally a top-five priority.
* You have enough credibility for Pat to set time to learn more.

Depending on how your team is structured, you might set a call with the AE right here, or you might set more time with Pat to ask additional qualification questions.

OK, but how do we physically open the call?

> Pat, this is Taylor with Alpha Corp. Did I catch you at a good time?

Go back to Pat's schedule above. Extrapolate that to every day of the week, every week of the year. When do you think a "good time" would be? Maybe never!

Also, so many people use this line that when you say it, the prospect hears, "WARNING! THIS IS A SALES CALL!"

> Pat, this is Taylor with Alpha Corp. How are you today?

What response to this question helps you or Pat? You might hear the following:

* "I'm great.": Now you can say what you should have said in your opening statement!
* "I'm having a terrible day.": What do you say to that?

* **"Who is this?"**: Now you can say what you should have said in your opening statement!

Here is a better example of an opener:

Pat, this is Taylor with Alpha Corp. In forty-five seconds I can explain why I've called and you can tell me if it makes sense to have a further discussion. Is that OK?

Own the fact that it's a cold call! By asking for an explicit amount of time, the prospects know what they are getting into and will be more willing to engage. Ask for as much time as you need, but the closer to thirty seconds, the better.

During your X seconds, you might say something like the following:

We help companies who experience [Pain 1], [Pain 2], and [Pain 3]. We've recently worked with other CFOs at companies similar to yours and [describe impact]. Based on what you've heard, do you think it makes sense to have a further conversation?

It's like fishing. Your call is the cast. This intro is your bait. Either the fish (the prospect) bites, or it doesn't, and you move on to the next one. If you have ever gone fishing, however, you know that once you set the hook, there are a lot of things you can do to lose the fish before it's in the boat.

But let's back up the fishing analogy real quick. You might be thinking, "How can I pick the three pain points to discuss when I haven't learned anything about the prospect yet? I thought I am supposed to ask open-ended questions?"

Open-ended questions are great if you have thirty minutes, but if you have thirty seconds, you need to pick a bait, cast it, and see if the fish bites. Again, think about the following in the context of Pat's day:

Pat, this is Taylor with Alpha Corp. Can I ask you what is your biggest pain point related to X that you have today?

Is there any chance that Pat will want to engage with this type of conversation at this point? Does Pat have any reason to trust you?

Become a Master of Relevance

There are several ways to craft a call script, but one universal truth prevails: make it relevant! When you call prospects, they care about one thing:

What's in it for me?

Good SDRs know the relevant messaging available to them and can dynamically reference it when relevant prospect pain surfaces. Figure 8.2 outlines what might be considered relevant and irrelevant.

Relevant	Irrelevant
A case study showing how your company helped someone similar to the prospect solve a problem that the prospect probably has.	Bragging about where your founders went to college.
News events that could compel the prospect to be interested in your product.	Digging into specific product features before finding prospect pain.
Stating: *"Typically when [Job Title]s download XYZ White Paper, they are frustrated by [a pain point you solve for companies like them related to the white paper], is that the case with you?"*	Asking: *"Do you have any questions about XYZ White Paper that you downloaded?"*

Figure 8.2: Examples given to prospects must be relevant.

Relevance can exist at either the company or the persona level. For example:

* A manufacturing company probably cares how you have worked with other manufacturing companies.
* A manufacturing company probably does not care that Facebook is a customer.
* The CIO at a manufacturing company might care that you sold to the CIO at Southwest Airlines.
* The CIO at Facebook probably does not care that you sold to the marketing operations manager at a manufacturing company.

Internal Referrals & Mapping

We introduced the concept of account-based selling (ABS) in chapter 4, and here you can see it in action. The person you initially reach out to often is not the right person to lead the evaluation of your product. You might have accidentally reached out to the wrong person, or you might have done so on purpose. Strategies for purposefully setting yourself up for referrals include:

* **Selling High**: If you think the CXO will care about what you do, start there and have him or her push you down to someone on his or her team, giving you credibility since a senior executive thought what you have to say is interesting. However, some middle managers hate it when salespeople use this tactic, so tread lightly.
* **Building Champions**: If someone in the company is likely to advocate on your behalf internally, it might be smart to start there and let that person coach you on how to sell to his or her organization.

* **Avoiding Friction**: Some personas are hard to reach, either because they are always underwater, or just don't like speaking with salespeople. If you have one persona who is easier to reach, and would care at least a little about your product, it might make sense to start there and ask for an internal referral.

Teamwork!

SDRs should share successes and failures with one another and update their scripts accordingly. If something specific is working for SDR A, it will probably also work for SDR B. Trade stories and make the whole company better!

Again, when we say "script," we mean the points to hit on during a call. Don't ignore this section just because we used the s-word!

Voicemail

Using voicemail is hit or miss. While it's something you should experiment with, you won't hit your quota by leaving awesome voicemails. Here are some principles to consider:

* **Shorter is Better**: Messages are returned in the inverse of their length. No one is going to listen to your two-minute voicemail.
* **Automate Them**: If your dialing software does not let you push a button and pick a voicemail to leave, you need better dialing software. Avoid wasting your time repeating the same message all day…that's "fake work."
* **Consider Them Marketing**: Even if no one ever calls you back, hearing your name, your company's name, and your short value prop is a marketing touch.

* **Prepare to be Ghosted**: Some prospects will figure out you're a salesperson and mark you as "do not answer" in their phone.

If someone starts ghosting you on the phone, try a different channel, such as social media or direct mail. Just don't be a stalker...no one buys from stalkers.

Getting Past the Gatekeeper

C-Level prospects will often have an executive assistant or a chief of staff. You might assume that these people are there to block vendors, but that's not the case. They are there to optimize the executive's calendar, and if you can help solve an important problem, they will let you through the gate!

Note that there is a difference between the executive assistant and the receptionist. The receptionist is not as close to the executive and could try to block all vendors, so there are several tactics that you can use to get around receptionists, including:

* **Time of Day:** Some people say timing doesn't matter. If it does in your business, try early mornings, lunchtime, or early evenings when the gatekeeper might be away.
* **Reference Prior Action**: If your prospect reached out to you (via the web, trade show, and so on), let the gatekeeper know.
* **Social Proof**: Create "fear of missing out" (FOMO) by referencing the fact that other companies similar to your prospect are working with you. However, keep it relevant. Don't always reference the same companies if their use case is not similar to that of your prospect.

Whatever you do, be respectful and ethical. Many executives will judge you based on how you treat their staff.

A Note on Fraud

Some companies use localization technology to trick prospects into thinking that they are calling from a local number. Call it what you will…we consider that fraud.

If the *very first experience* prospects have with your company is SDRs trying to trick them into thinking that they are local when they're not, how do you think the prospects will feel? They might think that:

* The SDR will trick them into meeting with the AE to hit their quota.
* The AE will make them think the product is a good fit when it is not.
* The legal team will bury adverse terms and conditions in the contract.

See what we have started here? We have included more on ethics in chapter 15, but the simple test is as follows…If you don't want:

[Your name] did [X]

on the cover of the *New York Times*…then don't do [X].

Maximillian's Mishaps

* Says "Um" frequently. Sheryl Sandberg said it best, *"When you say 'um' every third word, it makes you sound stupid."*

* Goes with the flow and allows the prospect to lead the conversation in hopes that the prospect with "sell himself."
* Memorizes one piece of customer evidence (case study, whitepaper, or statistic) and uses it in every situation, regardless of relevance.
* Uses "local presence dialing" to trick prospects into thinking they are receiving a local call in hopes of increasing his connection rate.
* Sells to the gatekeeper in hopes that they will grease the skids for the buyer.
* Sells to voicemail, because after all—it's a captive audience!

Boss's Brain

* **Conversions:** Convert conversations, whether inbound or outbound, into qualified opportunities for your AE.
* **Call Mechanics:** Demonstrate an ability to have natural conversation devoid of robotic qualification checklists, words like "great," "cool," "awesome," "totally," "definitely," or "absolutely," and tone-deaf responses to pain statements. If you are using a script, master it so that prospects are none the wiser.

Chapter 9

● ● ●

Social Media

Chapter Goal: Become a master of LinkedIn in just twenty minutes a day and learn principles you can extend to other social platforms.

*L*ast week, after appearing as a guest on a well-known podcast, *Alex received five inbound leads that instantly converted to opportunities. Not inbound to the company...inbound to her, personally. She directly attributed this success to her social selling skills. Her colleagues were stunned and frustrated.*

> *Lazy Leonard: How do you get invited to be on podcasts and guest-write blog posts?*

> *Feature-Loving Fran: Yeah, we started at the same time, and I share our product updates on LinkedIn all the time...social selling just doesn't work for me.*

> *Alex: *laughing* Promoting our product updates won't get you followers. You need to engage with people. I have a*

daily social-selling checklist, and in less than two hours a
week, I have built quite the following.

Twenty Minutes on LinkedIn

Ready...set...let's "social sell!"

OK, not so fast. Let's make a plan first. Figure 9.1 is an example of
a "social-selling checklist" that we will use to structure the rest of
this section.

COMPLETED?	ACTIVITY
	FOLLOW 3 PROSPECTS
	COMMENT ON ONE RELEVANT POST
	LIKE ONE RELEVANT POST
	PUBLISH ONE UPDATE
	CONNECT WITH NEW PROSPECTS & INCLUDE PERSONAL NOTE
	[WEEKLY] PUBLISH ONE LONG-FORM POST

Figure 9.1: A daily LinkedIn checklist

We will now examine the principles behind each item on this
checklist. Since LinkedIn is frequently making updates, we will not
include screenshots here because they will rapidly become outdat-
ed. However, we have made a video showing a full walk-through at
SalesDevelopmentBook.com.

Follow Three Prospects

Do not connect with them. Follow them. Here is the difference in
the prospects' minds:

Connect: They get an e-mail, in-app notification, and (hopefully) a personal message from you. Since you have not met, they think, "Here comes another salesperson to tell me why their stuff is awesome and I need it!"

Follow: They still get a notification that someone has followed them, but you cannot send private messages, so they are not waiting for an imminent pitch.

You might be thinking:

Wait, if I just follow them, I can't message them. If I don't message them, I won't get a meeting, and then I'll miss my quota!

We are playing the long game here. You should only be using LinkedIn if your prospects also use it frequently, so assuming they do, once you follow them, their activity will show up on your feed. That's where the next part comes into play.

Comment on One Relevant Post

Now that you are following people, their activity will show up on your feed. If you are not seeing anything worthy of engaging with, you can also visit prospect profile pages and see their recent activity right there!

The goal here is to find an article, post, or comment someone else has made where you can add some value. Maybe you can help someone answer a question, or you can take a point of view on an issue.

Whatever you do, don't try to sell your product in a comment. Don't even mention it! Seriously. You know how you feel when you are having a nice dinner, you are deep in conversation, and some street vendor walks up trying to sell you roses? That's exactly who you are in this case if you talk about your product.

Great comments typically have the following structure:

* [Poster Name], I agree! I've also noticed [something interesting that isn't self-promotional].
* [Poster Name], I see where you're coming from, but I've had a different experience. What I've seen is [what you've seen that's interesting and not self-promotional].

Bad comments include:

* Anything self-promotional. Yes, we're beating a dead horse here, but *please* take this point to heart.
* Simple comments like "I agree" or "Yes!" are not meaningful. You are doing nothing to show that you are a smart person who has expertise on the topic.
* Tagging other people to make it look like you have a strong network. If you want to tag a friend, fine, but it's better to message them a link to the post and let them comment if they want.

If you continuously post smart things that are not self-promotional, people in your market will start to follow you! And guess what, when you cold call them, they will already have an opinion of you... hopefully that you are an expert and can help!

Like a Post

Liking is the easiest thing to do but also the least effective. When done wrong, it can derail your other social efforts.

When you like something, the person gets an alert that you liked what they said. However, if multiple people like it, they will only get one alert, so your name will not stand out unless they click and scroll through all of the people who liked the post.

The place where liking can hurt you is when it comes to the visibility of your comments on other people's posts. Remember how you thought hard and wrote something relevant? Well, everything you like or comment on will show up in your connections' feed, so each additional like dilutes the total impact of your thoughtful comments.

We are not saying that you shouldn't like things, but overliking will distract from the points you're trying to make in your comments.

Publish an Update

When we say "update," we are talking about the place at the top of your feed where you can share something...very similar to how Facebook works. There are several things you can do here:

* Share a link
* Write a short comment
* Write a long comment (up to 1,250 characters)
* Publish a video
* Publish a long-form post (more on that in the next section)

Link sharing can be helpful, but make sure you also add some value. Ideally, what you write in addition to the link is similar to what you would write when commenting on another post. That makes sense, since you are essentially commenting on the article that is being shared. Simply pasting a link to some announcement your company made is self-promotional and will just create noise in your followers' feeds.

Your short and long updates should also be compelling and interesting. Again, it's tempting to promote your business here, but don't. You will lose followers, and people won't engage. Here are some examples of updates:

You likely agree with our good examples, but at first glance, you might not agree with the first and last bad ones. As for "happy Monday!," what if everyone in your network said that? LinkedIn would be *ruined*. Also, are you somehow uniquely qualified to be the person who wishes people a happy Monday? Our point extends beyond this specific example to anything that's a generic platitude that adds no specific value and will leave no one disagreeing.

As for the last example in the list above, it's pretty obvious that you are catfishing for business. That's annoying, but the more annoying

Good Updates	Bad Updates
I just learned about [topic]. It's really interesting because [compelling reason].	Happy Monday, everyone!
A rant about what drives you crazy, as long as you are specific but don't specifically throw anyone under the bus.	Publicly shaming anyone. It's OK to use specific examples, but don't make something an attack.
Anything that receives positive likes or comments from your market, and anything that stirs up a little bit of constructive debate.	Who are the best [Name of Persona You Sell To] in the tech industry?

Figure 9.2: Be interesting and engaging!

part is that every person who comments will receive an alert every time anyone else comments. *Then*, one or two people who are of that persona will start telling all of their friends to list them in the post, so it artificially gets out of control. Tagging a bunch of people in a post is social spam. Encouraging a bunch of people to tag others makes you "an accessory to social spam," which could become a misdemeanor someday.

Connect with Prospects

In addition to just following people, it's also good to connect with them from time to time. If you have had a two-way conversation of any substance, connect and send a personal note. Once you are connected, they will see all of your posts and comments, so be sure to maintain quality!

If you think a prospect is a great fit and you want to schedule a meeting, it's a better idea to send them an InMail instead of a connection request. The cool thing about InMails is that they offer the "LinkedIn Double-Tap," which means the recipient receives an e-mail *and* an in-app alert until they read your message. You get two touches for the price of one!

If you are already connected and want to reengage, consider endorsing them for a skill or sending a direct message. Since you are already connected, the message will not cost you an InMail credit!

Publish a Long-Form Post

Blogging time! If you are good at writing, this topic might come easy. If writing is not your forte, it will be challenging, but to become an effective executive you will need to learn how to write at some point!

Do your thing and be creative. There is no formula that says you must "write like X." However, here are some guidelines:

* Read other posts and pick out styles you wish to emulate.
* Break up your paragraphs. People like to skim, so limiting your paragraphs to two to six lines each is ideal.
* Open strong! You will lose your reader if you don't hook them out of the gate.
* Be interesting! You are not writing a formal essay for class. Have some fun.
* Close strong.
* Do not be self-promotional, though it is acceptable to have a relevant call to action at the end.

These posts can be a lot of work, so don't let them distract you from your core job; you might want to limit your writing to once per week or once per month. You might also want to have a friend or mentor review your first few posts to offer candid feedback. If you sound like an idiot or aren't interesting, you will do more harm than good.

Nineteen Minutes Later...

Before you know it, your twenty minutes on LinkedIn will be up! Those who practice quality and consistency will eventually build strong networks that help them get their foot in the door. Imagine what happens if one of your prospects posts the following on their feed:

I'm excited to be a new customer of [Your Company]! [Your Name] did an amazing job showing me the light, and we're pumped to see what [Your Company] can do for us!

Wow! How's that for social proof? Your prospect likely knows several people in his or her industry, and many will see what was written above. They will also see your intelligent, insightful, and non-self-promotional comment that you leave below!

Your Profile is an Inbound Marketing Asset

One of the most overlooked tools on social sites is the profile. As of the day this chapter was written, Cory Bray had 6,381 people view his LinkedIn profile in the last ninety days. Instead of just putting his job title and company names, he has turned it into an inbound marketing page for his books and company.

Oh, and this is the one place on LinkedIn where it's OK to be (tastefully) self-promotional. By clicking on your profile link, people have opted in to learning about *you*. Let's look at a few things you can do in order to at least give yourself a shot at converting leads from your LinkedIn profile.

Headline Image: Change the default background image to something related to your business.

Title (Headline): Your title is shown in your posts and comments, so make it something that will attract people to your profile. It should be interesting to people in your market, and you can use the 'I' key on your keyboard to separate statements. Once you have something you like, see how it appears on posts and comments before finalizing.

Summary: Shows up right below your headline and allows you to give a quick update or make an offer to your reader.

Experience: Think about your buyer here. If you love your job and want to sell your product, write something compelling that likely outlines the pain you solve or relevant customer stories. If you are looking for a job, your "buyers" are your next potential bosses, so tell them what they want to hear!

Experience (Prior Jobs): Make sure what you highlight from prior jobs 1) is true and 2) tells a story that leads up to what you do today.

Education: Make sure your most impressive education shows up in the headline. However, if you paid for a one-week certificate from Harvard, don't say you went to Harvard! Losers do that.

Recommendations: If you are looking for a job, these are very helpful. If you are trying to sell something, not so much. Over time, try to build your recommendations, but don't spend too much time here.

As with other types of communication, if you keep everything here specific, concise, and accurate, you will be in great shape!

Other Social Platforms

While other social platforms are technically different, the same principles we outlined above still apply. One exception is Twitter, where it is perfectly normal to tweet multiple times a day, though you should use a social automation tool to avoid wasting time on Twitter.

Maximillian's Mishaps

* Uses self-promotional language in comments and posts.
* Publicly attacks other people and companies.
* Posts about his dog sometimes. His company sometimes. His college sometimes. Whatever he feels at the moment.
* Tags several people he doesn't really know in posts to increase engagement and reach.

Boss's Brain

* **Brand:** Maintain consistent messaging, so there is no doubt about what your company does and how it helps customers.
* **Reach:** Maximize the number of people in your target market who know about your company.
* **Responsibility:** Post responsibly as though you are representing your company on a highway billboard. You are a reflection of your company
* **Conversion:** Turn social touches into qualified opportunities. Your job is to pass good leads to your AE…not become a social media star.

Chapter 10

● ● ●

Other Prospecting Tactics

Chapter Goal: Identify lead generation tactics you can use in addition to e-mail, phone, and social media. Good SDRs never complain that they don't have enough leads.

Alex schedules more meetings than anyone else on the SDR team. Is it because she has a better understanding of her buyer, her market, and talks about her product in a way that resonates with prospects? Maybe, but that's not the only reason.

Many of the outbound calls Alex makes are following up on a direct mail piece she sent to prospects.

Instead of a generic "I want to schedule time with you" call, her calls look something like the following:

   Prospect: *Hello?*

   Alex: *This is Alex with ExampleCorp.*

Prospect: Alex! Thank you so much for the book you sent! I've been meaning to call you back! That was very creative!

True story. This tactic works when personal relevance is applied.

Direct Mail

We *love* direct mail. Why? Because it works!

After we wrote *The Sales Enablement Playbook*, one SDR reached out and asked if he could buy copies from us at a discount and send them to prospects. He paid less than four dollars per book, sent one to fifty target accounts, and connected with forty-one of them within a month. Compared to previous tactics, he claimed that this approach, "was like shooting fish in a barrel."

Think about it…what is more likely to resonate with your buyer?

1. A call from a stranger asking for some time?
2. *Another* e-mail?
3. A voicemail?
4. A copy of a book relevant to the prospect's job, with a hand-written note providing context for the outreach?

Pick your answer. Now, ask a couple of your execs…people who are constantly hit up by SDRs from other companies. What do they think?

That Sounds Expensive!

One of the challenges SDRs face is moving from a "personal money" mind-set to a "business money" mind-set. While the thought of spending $1,000 on an experiment in your personal life might cause your blood pressure to spike, such an investment with "business money" is closer to $0 than anything else.

Let's go with the book example and break things down:

* Book Cost: $4.00
* Shipping Cost (USPS Media Mail): $2.63
* Office Supplies (Envelope, Sticky Note, Pen, etc.): $0.10
* Total Cost: $6.73

If you send fifty, your cost is less than $350. As an SDR in San Francisco, you likely cost your company more than this amount for *one day*. This amount is literally nothing...just an experiment.

A book might not be the right option, but something exists that will resonate with your prospect much better than a random call. Use your noggin and be creative. *Then* you call them!

If you want to be an executive someday, one of the things you need to learn is how to get a budget for projects, show preliminary success, and expand the scope. There is no better way to start to build this skill set than on direct mail campaigns this quarter!

Texting

Some SDR managers say no to texting. When we hear this statement, it's less about the act of texting and more about how much they trust their team to be businesspeople. If your SDR team still thinks they live in the frat house, then maybe texting is a bad idea.

But if you are a team of businesspeople, it should at least be considered as part of the outreach cadence.

If you call a prospect's cell phone and get their voicemail, a text might be the right next move. Since texts are more visible than voicemail, you are more likely to get a quick response.

Networking

Your network is your strongest long-term asset. Treat it like a garden...plant seeds, nurture it, don't overharvest, and eventually, you will have something really special.

You can leverage your network for general advice and introductions to potential job opportunities or sales prospects. However, the probability that any one person has a connection to a qualified prospect or job is very low, so you might not see any results here until your network becomes quite large.

Here are some tips when it comes to networking:

* Do your homework. Who do you want to talk to?
* Identify a quantifiable goal.
* Know your elevator pitch, and a ten-second intro.
* Work the room.
* Make sure that networking doesn't become notworking.

Trade Shows

We *love* trade shows. They are the one place on earth where senior execs from your prospect companies come to talk to you. OK...they are exploring new technology and what they might be missing out on, but *you* are part of that.

As an SDR, you will not be involved in all aspects of a trade show, but since so many companies are executing poorly these days, we wanted to give you a short playbook that might help you drive change at your company.

Before the Show

The hardest part is to determine your strategy, including which sponsorship packages to purchase. For most events, your marketing team will have the ability to buy:

* **Booth Space**: A physical presence on the exhibit hall floor (or in the lobby for a smaller event) that allows you to promote your business.
* **Meeting Rooms**: Your home away from home where salespeople and execs can meet with prospects.
* **Speaking Time**: Some speakers are paid, some are invited to speak for free, and some must pay to appear on stage. Relevant vendors typically fit into the last category.
* **Branding**: Have your logo displayed on the event or sponsor a specific activity, such as happy hour.

Booth space is a lot of fun. People walk by, you grab their attention, and either disqualify them fast or propose next steps. It's like making a bunch of rapid in-person cold calls with people who are at least somewhat likely to be interested in what you have to say.

The mistakes many people make while working a booth include:

* Focus on the quantity of badges scanned or business cards collected.
* Have some gimmick that does not offer real value to the prospect.
* Goofing off and not paying attention.

There's nothing wrong with focusing on quantity if you are segmenting your leads by potential fit at both the company and persona level. Figure 10.1 outlines some examples of what we've seen on trade-show floors.

Good Moves	Bad Moves
Attract attention with something fun and interesting, such as a wheel to spin and win prizes, *and* use the "fun time" to ask one qualifying question that can then be parlayed into a conversation with good prospects.	Have your team stand around and say, "Can I scan you for charity?" That's French for, "I'm going to e-mail spam you, and if you don't opt in, you're a bad person." How on earth is that "business?"
Attract people with gender-neutral toys for children. Many execs are on the road away from their families, and when Little Taylor gets a prize, that makes business travel more tolerable. Again, *know your buyers!*	Have a drawing for something everyone already has. First, not everyone trusts drawings. Second, how many people need a tablet and don't have one?
Help your prospect learn something relevant to both them and you. We like to make *The Sales Enablement Playbook* free on Kindle for trade shows and hand out flyers showing people how to get it.	Do nothing. If everyone else is being fun and engaging, no one is going to come to your booth if you are not doing anything interesting.

Figure 10.1: Trade-show preparation do's and don'ts.

Since the exhibit hall floor is a great place to engage prospects, it's wise for SDRs to figure out who will be in attendance and encourage them to either stop by the booth, come to a speaking session, or book some time in the private meeting room. Ways to determine who will be there include:

* **Ask Them**: A great question to ask prospects during a first call is, "By the way, what events do you typically attend each year?"
* **Sponsor List**: If they are sponsoring an event, you know your prospects (or at least one of their colleagues) will be there.
* **Data Vendor**: If your data provider has conferences as part of their offering, that could be a good start. However, be careful with these types of products and triple-check accuracy against a known clean list before spending money. Some are known to have dirty data.

Some companies will ask the SDR to schedule a time with the prospect to stop by the booth, but again, think about this tactic from your buyers' perspective. They are taking time off work, leaving their families, catching up with colleagues from all over the place, and likely attending sessions on a whim…is it reasonable for them to work around your schedule? Instead, give them a really compelling reason to come say hi on their terms. If they are a great prospect, maybe do something special like invite them to a nice dinner with your execs.

During the Show

At the trade show, the number-one driver of success is *focus*. That means:

* Don't text your friends.
* Forget about social media, other than posting relevant LinkedIn updates.
* Put an out-of-office response on your e-mail.

Sales Development

It's pathetic how many people sit at their booths with their faces in their screen. There is no reason to be there if you are going to play on your phone. Instead, spend the entire time on the floor engaging prospects.

Some people walking by your exhibit will stop on their own, but others will need to be lured. Here are some tactics that work:

* **Make Eye Contact**: Once you lock eyes with people, there is a good chance they will listen to the next thing you say.
* **Short Pitch**: If you are giving away a book, say "Free book." If you want to show a short demo of X, say, "Fifteen seconds to learn about X?"
* **Be Nice**: A lot of people will still blow you off, but don't take it personally. Getting an attitude will harm your brand.

Once you engage someone, the next move is to either set a next step or disqualify them as fast as possible. If they are not a fit, politely bow out of the conversation. If you think they might be a fit, grab a couple of pieces of information and set a follow-up task.

When dealing with business cards, especially if you are depositing them into a fishbowl, one tactic is to bend (dog-ear) corners to indicate whether the prospect is a fit or not.

* **No Bends**: Not a fit
* **One Bend**: Interesting
* **Two Bends**: Very good prospect
* **Three Bends**: Amazing prospect
* **Four Bends**: Save this one for your unicorn

129

The final point is to "sprint through the finish line." Don't get lazy while there is still an opportunity to talk with prospects. Sure, you might have been at the booth all day and feel tired, but that last hour has much more potential than an hour of cold calling when you get back to your desk the next week.

After the Show

The postshow follow-up is the make-or-break point for SDRs. Sooo many companies get this part wrong. Figure 10.2 outlines some of what we have seen.

Good Moves	Bad Moves
The person who talked to the prospect at the show is the one who follows up. If it was an exec, he or she can introduce you in the first e-mail; then you take over from there.	The marketing team sends the same e-mail blast to all prospects, without mentioning any specific conversations.
The proposed next step in the follow-up accounts for the prospect's persona and their company's market segment (i.e., it is relevant!).	Your prospect receives an e-mail or call saying he or she should take action that makes no sense in the context of their business.

Figure 10.2: Trade-show follow-up do's and don'ts.

Postshow spikes in lead volume are overwhelming and can result in low-quality outreach. Time management becomes critical, and you should focus on the highest-quality leads first.

Referral System

If they are honest, most salespeople will tell you that their referral system is:

"I sometimes ask for referrals when I think about it and feel that a 'no' won't throw a deal off track or hurt my feelings."

Salespeople will often say, "I want to wait until someone is a satisfied customer before asking…," or "Customers who love us will give referrals without asking…" The important thing to remember here is that a referral is *not* a recommendation. It is just an opportunity to speak to someone who fits specifically articulated demographic criteria.

A systematic approach to referrals will yield real results. A referral system includes:

*   Who to ask for a referral (everyone)
*   When to ask (early and often)
*   Clozing the loop with the person who made the referral

Imagine how much easier your job would be if your current prospects gave birth to new prospects? Or if you worked with your teammates (specifically in customer success) to farm referrals out of people who love your company?

What to Say

When you first contact a referral, the conversation is just like a cold call:

Hi Jennifer, it's Alex from ExampleCorp. That name probably doesn't sound familiar, does it? Reggy from Acme thought it might make sense for us to connect. I can explain why I'm calling in about thirty seconds, and you can decide if it makes sense to keep talking. Would that be OK?

What do you do in that thirty seconds? Your elevator pitch! Referral calls are only slightly warmer than cold. If you are able to get an introduction (via e-mail or otherwise) from the referrer, then you don't have to do the name-and-company dance and can dive right into the elevator pitch. Remember, your "pitch" is not on features and benefits, but the pain you solve!

Do the Math!

If you get twenty-five leads the "old-fashioned way," you have twenty-five leads. Now, imagine that 40 percent of the prospects you speak with give you a good referral. Now you have thirty-five leads, right? Wrong!

You also get referrals from the referrals, so think about it:

Raw Leads: 25
First-Order: 10
Second-Order: 4
Third-Order: 1

Instead of having twenty-five leads, you now have forty. But it doesn't stop there! What if a prospect gives you more than one? Wow...this math can get out of control. Seriously, because you don't have twenty-five leads, you have way more:

Raw Leads: 250
First-Order: 100
Second-Order: 40
Third-Order: 16
Fourth-Order: ~7
Fifth-Order: ~3

That's almost another 170 leads on top of the original 250! Wow! Do yourself a favor and take advantage of the opportunity outlined in figure 10.4.

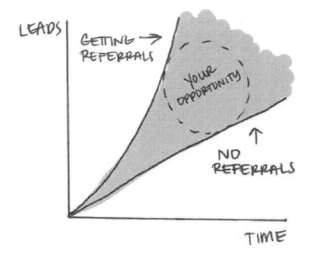

Figure 10.4: Referrals exponentially increase the number of leads you can generate.

Use Referrals to Make a Splash

Your fellow SDRs are probably not asking everyone they speak with for a referral. There are no guarantees, but this *single tactic* might be enough to put you at the top of your company's leaderboard. After your referral plan is humming along, you can use its success to demonstrate why you are ready for a bigger role in your company.

Lost-Deal Analysis

Regardless of how awesome your company is, you have lost a lot of deals. In fact, you have probably lost way more than you have won.

On the surface, that might be frustrating, but think about it...there is opportunity, since a lot has likely changed since you lost the deal:

* The product is better.
* You have more customer success stories.
* Messaging has improved.

The cool thing about sales is that "no" is temporary. The deals you lost likely fit into one of the three following categories:

* **Dead:** These just went dark, and you have no idea if they have solved their problem.
* **Delayed Decision**: These people have not even solved the problem yet!
* **Bought Elsewhere**: Did it work out as expected?

Each of these situations provide an opportunity for reengagement when you have a better product with improved social proof and better messaging...so why not see if you can convert these lost deals to new opportunities? Hopefully you have accurate information in your CRM and can tie exactly why you lost to why you might have a better shot this time, given how things have changed.

Maximillian's Mishaps

* Relies exclusively on email and doesn't think outside of the box.
* Thinks that $1,000 is a ton of money and will not ask for budget for pet projects.
* Hangs out at networking events and on chat channels, but never converts business.

* Texts friends from the tradeshow floor.
* Either doesn't ask for referrals, or asks weak questions like, "Do you know anyone else like you who I could talk to?"
* Waits for "proof points" before asking a customer to refer business.

Boss's Brain

* **Building Pipeline**: Constantly source leads. Without leads, there is no revenue. Without revenue, there is no company.
* **Smart Experiments**: Identify prospecting experiments that might have impactful results. Be creative and be prepared to support your assumptions, defend a budget, and execute on a plan. However, don't get discouraged if you are sent back to the drawing board.
* **Efficiency**: Demonstrate your ability to optimize every channel. Referrals are a great example of how to produce stronger results with potentially low-hanging fruit.

Chapter 11

• • •

Objection Handling

Chapter Goal: Master techniques used to respond to prospects' objections and turn their resistance into a potential opportunity.

Feature-Loving Fran: Hey Alex, can you help me with something? I'm having a lot of conversations, but they aren't converting to meetings with my AE because I'm getting killed with objections. I have talked to the product team and think my responses are good, but they aren't working. Are there types of prospects I should talk to who won't have all of these objections?

Alex smiles. She has seen her colleague provide direct responses to objections on the phone and get frustrated after hanging up.

Alex: I actually like objections. In their absence, I don't know exactly what the prospect wants to talk about, but the minute they start throwing objections, it's clear where the conversation should head.

Fran: Really?

Alex: Yeah, and instead of responding directly, I ask clarifying questions, get to the bottom of their concern, and always try to look for pain that we can solve. That way we are talking about issues relevant to them, but I'm able to still control the conversation.

Question-Based Objection Handling

If you went to school in the United States, you know that when asked a question, all the people who think they have the right answer shoot their hands up in pursuit of the "gold star," and the person who the answers a question with a question is branded a smart-ass. As a result, the comfortable way to handle a prospect's objection is with a direct answer.

Prospect: *"Your product is too expensive."*

Direct Answer: *"Most of our customers find us quite affordable at $50K/year."*

Ouch...good luck convincing your prospects that all of a sudden they are wrong and you are right.

Here is another approach:

Prospect: *"Your product is too expensive."*

Answer 1: *"I hear your concern. Can you help me understand a little more about your financial considerations?"*

Answer 2: *"Do you mind helping me understand what type of budget you've allocated to this project? And if none has* *been allocated, what range would you be comfortable seeking to make a purchase?"*

Answer 3: *"It's always helpful to understand context when talking about pricing. Are there specific products in a different price range that ours is being compared against?"*

The last one is our favorite. Or more simply put, "expensive compared to what?" Thanks, J. B.

An objection is an opportunity to uncover more pain. You will not learn anything from answering their question directly, and worse, you can make unfounded assumptions that move the conversation in the wrong direction.

"Expensive" is relative. Tell a group of friends that you took an "expensive" vacation last summer and you will find different interpretations that could range from a trip to the Jersey Shore to a private jet around the world.

Hilmon once spoke to a prospect who began the conversation by saying, "I have heard that working with you can be expensive!" Hilmon replied, "Is that a good or a bad thing?" The prospect said, "Well if you're expensive...you must be the best. I want the best."

Objections Are Welcome!

Why do we dread objections? Maybe it's because the name evokes images of a lawyer in a movie rising in abject disagreement. For a lot of SDRs, it's because they are emotionally invested in the outcome of the call. A rejection becomes perceived as a personal insult or attack.

You're not good enough!

You have a lot of nerve!

You don't know what you're talking about!

Bringing up an objection is a natural way to ask key questions. For example, figure 11.1 outlines the likely meaning behind various objections a prospect might raise.

OBJECTION	POSSIBLE MEANING
THAT'S EXPENSIVE!	TELL ME MORE ABOUT YOUR PRICING
YOU DON'T INTEGRATE WITH SALESFORCE	HOW WILL OUR USERS ACCESS YOUR PRODUCT WITHIN THEIR WORKFLOW
I DON'T THINK YOU HAVE ALL THE FEATURES WE NEED TODAY	TELL ME ABOUT YOUR PRODUCT ROADMAP

Figure 11.1: Objections might mean more than what's on the surface.

Objections are not a sign that a prospect doesn't want to do business with you. Your reaction can either shut down the opportunity to peel back the layers of the onion or open an interesting dialogue.

Hear It Once, Never Again a Surprise
Whenever a new objection is heard:

* Write it down.
* Put it in a place where *everyone* can find it.
* Include responses that work. Not just answers, but responses that get a prospect talking, which will often tie back to your company's sales methodology.

* Provide tips on how to deliver the response (or clarifying question).
* Assign a shelf life to each entry. Competitors and products will change, so don't let the info go stale.
* Cloze the loop with feedback from everyone on what works and what doesn't.

Gaining Common Ground

One objection-handling tactic is to agree with the prospect and attempt to gain common ground. If a prospect has concerns about the product being too expensive, a good response might look something like this:

> *You're right; it is expensive. The first time I saw it, I was taken aback too. However, when I learned more about the product, the market, and what each customer gets, I realized that our product cuts spending in the long run. Should we keep talking?*

Gaining common ground with your prospect allows you to act as a trusted adviser and explore whether or not it makes sense to do business together. If you can work together in the sales process instead of being an adversary, things will end better for both of you. Notice the question at the end of the above statement. When handling objections, we want to be sure to keep the prospect talking and maintain control of the conversation.

Educators are taught that *"the person who asks the question controls the conversation."* Take heed and follow that axiom.

The Unspoken Objection

If you know something is going to be a problem for prospects based on one or more of their attributes, bring it up yourself.

For example, if your product doesn't integrate with Salesforce, and you know that might be a problem, put it on the table and use customer stories to explain how others have overcome this issue. If your product costs more than competitors', address the high price and discuss why others have found it to be a good deal. Being up-front and honest about the situation will help prospects feel comfortable with moving forward.

Remember though, as an SDR your job is to feed the AEs qualified leads, not to ferret out any possible objection. Do what you need to do, but only to get the prospect to the point where the AE can take over.

In cases where objections are clear deal killers, find that out earlier and avoid wasting time on someone who has no chance of becoming a customer. If it's a killer, don't fight it...just walk away graciously and focus on prospects who are a good fit.

Maximillian's Mishaps

* Feels personally attacked and gets defensive when he hears a prospect's objection.
* Avoids senior-level prospects because they are often analytical and full of objections.
* Does not discuss common objections and responses with teammates, so he's constantly reinventing the wheel.

* Hides from potential problem issues in the sales process instead of addressing them with the prospect before they surface.

Boss's Brain

* **Objection Handling**: Demonstrate an ability to turn objections into opportunities to explore how your product might be a good fit. Engage in challenging conversations and learn from them, instead of bailing out when the going gets tough.
* **Collaboration**: Be a contributor to the team's knowledge base. Whether through a formal system or technology, or in meetings and casual conversation, be sure that you increase overall team efficiency by sharing what's working and what isn't.

Chapter 12

● ● ●

Tools

Chapter Goal: Explore the tools available to you as an SDR and how they can be used to amplify your success.

At a recent sales development meetup, Alex was hanging out with SDRs from a few other companies, and they were talking about a typical day.

> *Tool-Happy Terri: Alex, I don't know how you can hit your quota without a full sales stack. I have eleven tools, and even I miss my number some months.*
>
> *Alex: Sales development success isn't about tools.*
>
> *Terri: But how do you stay efficient?*
>
> *Alex: Focus.*
>
> *Terri: But how do you make 150 calls, send 300 e-mails, and post on LinkedIn hourly without more tools?*

Alex: I don't.

Terri: What? How do you hit your number then?

Alex: I'm telling you…I do make lots of calls and send lots of e-mails, but they are all high-quality. And I'd never post on LinkedIn hourly!

Terri: Interesting. So how do you think about tools?

Alex: They enable quality at scale. That's it!

What is a Tool, Anyways?

In many sales organizations, leaders spot something they don't like, buy a tool that has roughly solved a similar problem for others in the past, and hope it works.

You wouldn't use a forklift unless you wanted to increase the efficiency of moving heavy objects from Point A to Point B. If you were unsure which object you wanted to move or didn't know where you wanted to move it, what good would buying a forklift do? Does anyone in your company currently know how to use or maintain a forklift? Have you built in the cost of fuel? Are you even certain that six months from now you will still need to move these objects? Or… are you just looking for a shiny new toy?

All tools do is amplify your efforts. If you are bad at making outbound calls, a power dialer will help you make more bad outbound calls. If your e-mails aren't good, an e-mail automation tool will help you send more bad e-mails. See the point?

In the start-up world, there is the concept of a "minimum viable product," or MVP. Before scaling, companies build a low-cost MVP and make sure it works. Like having your own start-up, everything you do that's customer-facing should have its own MVP so you can make sure that it works before automating anything! Some examples include:

* **E-mail Templates**: Send them to a small percentage of your list and see if they work before reaching out to everyone.
* **Call Frameworks**: If your message isn't converting, try something new.
* **Outreach Cadence**: Figure out how frequently you should ping prospects, and through which channels.
* **Social Selling**: Run experiments, but don't waste too much time here. Also, automating social can be perceived as inauthentic and fall flat.
* **Interns**: Interns are great, but if the task or project can be outsourced to someone on-demand, you might not have enough work to keep an intern engaged.

As an SDR, if something isn't working, just chill out and focus on your job. You can fill a day worrying about tools, but that won't help make you money and advance your career.

Tools for SDRs

There are several types of tools that are critical to the sales-development function. The only way to arrive at the right tool stack for your team is to answer these questions:

* What are all the problems we need to solve?
* Are these technology or analog (skill, quality, training) problems?

* What is the adverse impact if the problems are not solved?
* Do we have the ability to integrate this tool, train folks, and ensure adoption *now*?

As an SDR, you may be a heavy user of a sales technology stack and involved in the evaluation of tools.

Customer Relationship Management (CRM)

The CRM is the single source of truth for your sales team. There is a popular saying that sales leaders love:

If it's not in the CRM, it doesn't exist!

Here you will store the details captured for each lead so you and others have visibility into your pipeline. While you will have little influence on which CRM is used and how it is implemented, it's always smart to push back if people try to require additional fields, especially if the request is coming from someone who does not have a sales quota!

Data Provider

These vendors help you accomplish two main tasks:

Build Lists: Using attributes of your ideal customer profile (ICP), you can filter by company size, persona, technologies used, and so on. The fancy words vendors will use for these traits to help justify their value are firmographic, demographic, and technographic, respectively.

Enrich Data: If Pat Jones (pjones@getalphacorp.com) submits a form on your website and you only capture the e-mail address, it might be tough to find out more about Pat, right? That's where data enrichment vendors come into play. They can take the e-mail address and augment it in the CRM with phone number, address, title, and other data.

If SDRs are the engine of the lead-generation process, then data is the oil. Each time bad data is encountered, the SDR is either forced to do research or skips the current lead and moves on. Both are frustrating and lead to bad outcomes.

E-mail Cadence Tool

These products allow you to sequence e-mails to be sent at specific intervals over time. You can also set triggers to remove prospects from a sequence once something specific has happened, such as them replying to an e-mail.

Be careful not to let loose with e-mail sequences until you know your messaging resonates with prospects, which is why we discussed the concept of an MVP. It's better to test messaging on a small group than send something that doesn't resonate to your entire prospect list.

Power Dialer

Power dialers allow SDRs to press a single button to queue up a call. They are often built into e-mail cadence tools, thereby giving the SDR a one-stop-shop for reaching out to prospects.

There are also super-power-dialers that have humans dialing, talking to gatekeepers, and connecting to the contact behind the scenes; then the SDR jumps on when a prospect is there for a live conversation.

Video

If you don't use video as part of your prospecting efforts, you're missing out! Let's remove all constraints for a second. What's the *best* medium to use when interacting with prospects? There is one clear winner here:

In person. Face to face. With a whiteboard.

Text-based e-mail and telephone conversations are far removed from this utopia, but what if you embed a video in your e-mail? You are instantly:

More Personable: The prospect can see your face instead of just seeing your words.

Able to Show and Tell: Overlaying a small video of you on top of a screen of text or a product demo can help make your point, but in a personable way. See the "ClozeLoop" YouTube channel for examples.

Viral: If the person receiving your video wants to share what you had to say, what better way for you to spread the message around the company than your own words, delivered by you!

If you don't use video yet, start experimenting and see how it might work for you!

Learning Management Systems and Knowledge Management

The faster you learn all of the tactics used by your best salespeople, the faster you can become the best on your team! These products allow you to learn and reinforce concepts, as well as share what works with your colleagues.

Call Recording

If you play golf and don't regularly shoot in the seventies, record yourself at the driving range and watch it on the big screen. *Ouch!* It's one of the most embarrassing things you can do. Second only to listening to sales calls.

Things to listen for include:

* **Talk Time**: Did your prospect talk 60–70 percent of the time, or more? If not, you probably talked too much.
* **Pain**: Were you able to uncover real pain? When you found it, did you drill down, or prematurely move on to the next topic?
* **Relevance**: Were you able to cover what the prospect wanted to talk about?
* **Pivot**: Could you transition the conversation to cover other points important to you?
* **Posture**: Did you sound like an executive?
* **Filler Words**: Were you elegant, or was your speech full of "um's" and other filler words that make you sound dumb?
* **Happy Ears**: Did you get excited when you should have been skeptical?
* **Close**: Did you confidently close the next step?
* **Referral Ask**: Did you ask for a referral?

Cory Bray and Hilmon Sorey

You will identify several areas to improve, and if you're diligent about it, your skill level should improve rapidly.

Tools to record calls range from basic recording devices to products that analyze the details of the call and make coaching easier.

LiveChat

LiveChat can be placed on a company's website to communicate in real time with prospects. You can hop into a chat conversation, and if the person seems like a good lead, seamlessly transition to a phone call. The challenge is that quality will vary:

* **Unqualified Leads**: Unfortunately, unqualified leads like to talk and ask questions too...sometimes more than qualified leads. Master the art of identifying these people quickly and elegantly ending the conversation.
* **Junior People**: Individual contributors and middle managers (especially at big companies) often have checklists they're filling out when talking to vendors. These people might want to use live chat to play twenty questions (or "stump the chump" as some say). If that's the case, back up and see if you can get a call to discuss things at a high level first.
* **Great Leads**: Busy execs will pop onto your page and poke around to see if you might be a good fit. Be ready!

One benefit of LiveChat is that you can take a break to ask someone on your team a question. If a prospect has a technical issue, you can quickly consult a resource with more expertise, but without letting the prospect know you are interrupting the conversation to ask someone else. If a question arises that is too difficult to answer,

150

get the prospect's information and promise to get back to him or her quickly.

Remember that your job isn't to sit back and answer prospect questions; your job is to pass quality leads to AEs. That's why practicing a sales methodology is so critical…no matter what happens, you know how to maintain control of the sales process.

Maximillian's Mishaps

* Thinks he needs a tool for everything.
* Doesn't learn how to use his tools, and as a result, he's incredibly inefficient.
* Blames tools for his poor performance.
* Doesn't check automated emails for quality, so he ends up "amplifying the awful" and compounding the number of prospects who have a bad experience. He has become infamous on LinkedIn!

Boss's Brain

* **Technology Utilization**: Learn to effectively leverage technology to create process efficiency around the things you are already doing well. Automation for automation's sake is a recipe for disaster.
* **Quality**: Ensure that every touch with a prospect provides a competent and positive experience. Even those who are not going to buy from you will either become critics or evangelists of your message and process.

Chapter 13

● ● ●

Time Management

Chapter Goal: Get more done in the same amount of time!

*B*efore becoming an SDR, Alex prided herself on being a perfectionist and a multitasker. She received all A's in high school and had a near-perfect GPA in college. Long to-do lists were common, but not intimidating at all because she could jump from one item to the next and get everything done. However, after more than a year on the job as an SDR, she would not even recognize her former self.

Alex quickly realized that perfectionism and multitasking have no place in the world of sales development. She now focuses on work being "good enough" for the task at hand, and aggressively focuses on the highest-value activities.

> **Distracted Dino:** *Hey Alex, did you get that e-mail I sent you twenty minutes ago?*

> **Alex:** *No, I check e-mail every hour so I can focus. I have been making calls.*

Dino: I check it constantly in case something important comes in. You should too.

Alex: No offense, but you're also on pace to hit 60 percent of quota.

Prioritize Like a Pro

When observing successful senior executives at your company, you will notice that they are masters of prioritization. In fact, if you were good at school (and you probably were since you read books on your profession), their attitude at prioritization might be shocking. Here's why:

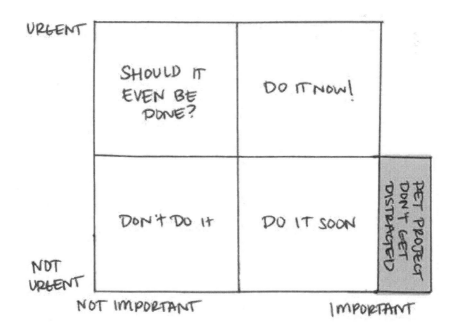

Figure 13.1: Prioritization is a critical skill for SDRs.

In school, we were *heavily* penalized for not doing an assignment. Failing to turn something in resulted in a zero, and heavily weighed on the end-of-term grade.

At work, we are *heavily* penalized for mediocre work. It's better to get one A+ and four zeros than it is to get five Bs.

Urgent and Important: Do It Now!

Step 1: Take a chill pill.

Almost every time we run across a "do-it-now" culture, the environment is toxic. While people are running around doing things frantically, tasks are half-done, employees become miserable, and after the miserable employees quit, things get worse. That's not to say that some tasks shouldn't be done immediately. Here are a few that come to mind:

* **Schedule a Call for the AE and Prospect**: Both the AE and prospect have busy schedules, so the minute you find a mutually agreeable time to talk, get it on the calendar.
* **Complete Follow-Up Request**: If a prospect asks a question you can't answer and it's worth answering, respond ASAP. Quick response times set you apart from the competition.
* **Respond to Execs**: If someone important at your company asks you a question, respond ASAP. Your response might be, "I can get that to you Thursday," but quick responses set you apart from your peers.

You might be thinking, "What about following up with inbound leads? Isn't that urgent and important?" Well, a lot of people will say it is, and they will even back it up with research saying that leads are X percent less likely to engage if you wait more than ten minutes to follow up. It makes us wonder, though:

> If someone will engage after ten minutes, but not after an hour, aren't they the same type of person who will be difficult to work with throughout the entire sales process? Should the sales team's time be focused on more responsive leads?

Sure, that's a hypothesis as well. Maybe it is critical to reach out the minute a lead comes in, and if that's what your company tells you, then do it! Also note that there is a difference between someone sending you a message saying, "I want to learn more about your product," and simply downloading a white paper. The former is obviously much more urgent.

Not Urgent, but Important: Do It Soon!

Successful SDRs spend the majority of their days in this quadrant. As a result, you will work on tasks that are important to you and your company, but you will not run around all day with your hair on fire.

These type of tasks include:

* Initial outreach to prospects
* Work your pipeline
* One-on-ones with your manager and AE (you have these, right?)
* Social media
* Research

* Check e-mail
* Update the CRM

Be careful with the last two. Responding to e-mails and updating the CRM can feel like accomplishments, but they're not. You need to find the right cadence for you, but it shouldn't be *right now*. The key in this quadrant is to schedule the activity on your calendar.

Urgent, but Not Important: Should It Even Be Done?

As an SDR, two of your top priorities are to make money and build skills for future positions. Every second you spend working on something that's not important, you are stalling progress toward these goals.

You are not in school anymore, so the name of the game isn't "do everything in front of you." However, you should get buy-in from your manager if you decide something isn't worth your time. It may not be important to you, but it might be important to the company. A small percentage of your time will be spent doing these types of tasks, and that's one of the reasons why you get paid.

Urgent-but-not-important tasks include:

* Responding to information requests from obviously unqualified leads
* Some internal meetings
* Some internal requests (like those that come across your chat application)

Just keep an eye out here. Shifting your focus from this quadrant to the two previously discussed can have a positive impact on your success.

Not Urgent and Not Important: Don't Do It!

Seriously, don't waste time here. It might feel good to check things off your list to feel like you're making progress, but instead of wasting your time, check out the section on negative goals in this chapter.

Pet Projects

At some point, you will find something you are passionate about, but falls slightly outside of your core job description. Here we have a "pet project." Examples in the SDR world include:

* **New Process**: Do you see inefficiency and have an idea how to fix it?
* **New Role**: Maybe having one person do all of the research instead of everyone doing research and making calls is a good move.
* **New Technology**: Can you make a current process more efficient with a new tool?

Successful pet projects can set you apart from your peers. Just be sure that you are hitting your goals consistently before you take on any pet projects!

Bracketing Your Day

Splitting up your day into brackets and focusing on one thing at a time allows you to put your full mind and energy behind the task at hand. It doesn't usually matter when you do things (well, don't make calls at 10:00 p.m.), it's more about the fact that you have a plan to focus and follow through on this plan. Figure 13.2 shows an example of a well-bracketed day.

	MONDAY	TUESDAY	WEDNESDAY	THURSDAY	FRIDAY
MORNING	MEETINGS	CALLS	CALLS	CALLS	CALLS
MID-DAY	CALLS	EMAILS	CALLS	EMAILS	RESEARCH
AFTERNOON	EMAILS	RESEARCH	EMAILS	RESEARCH	PLANNING
EVENING	GET AHEAD	GET AHEAD	GET AHEAD	GET AHEAD	GET AHEAD

Figure 13.2: Uninterrupted blocks of time lead to higher productivity.

The trick is to ensure your body's performance matches how you split up your activities. If you get groggy in the afternoon, try to make most of your calls in the morning...or change your lunch habits! If you handle inbound inquiries and need to jump on them quickly, figure out the time of day with the highest volume, and set aside another part of the day to follow up on existing leads.

If you find yourself constantly replying to each e-mail or chat message that comes in, there are likely some huge ways to increase your productivity!

The Concept of Negative Goals

Prospecting is hard. Anyone who says it's easy has never done it.

SDRs receive constant rejection, where even a 2 percent success rate can be considered successful. Who in the world can feel good about being rejected 98 percent of the time? Can you imagine that being a positive experience? One way to cope with constant rejection is to focus on "negative goals."

Imagine that you need to find fifty qualified leads per quarter (roughly four per week). Depending on your business, you might need to reach out to 2,500 people to achieve this goal. As a result, for every one win there are forty-nine losses...feels pretty terrible, eh? Here's where negative goals come in:

* Flip the goal from getting one yes to getting forty-nine nos.
* Each time the prospect says no, that's progress toward the goal, not a kick in the teeth.
* Eventually, someone will say yes, which is a *huge* win.

Some people will be able to tough it out through constant rejection, but often it takes a little more. Try negative goals; there's a good chance that you will be able to push yourself harder than you thought. Look at the impact on your day as shown in figure 13.3.

Figure 13.3: With negative goals, you're always winning!

How Many Hours Should I Work?

If your goal right now is work–life balance, skip this profession. We're not trying to change your mind; you do you. However, if your long-term goal is work–life balance while earning a ton of money and impacting your industry, then stick around.

Instead of stressing work–life balance, we like the following concept:

> *Your twenties are for learning, then your thirties and forties are for earning.*

There is a minimum skill set needed to move into high-paying jobs down the road. Failing to build a strong foundation early on can turn someone's career into a house of cards, where they are one event away from a major career setback. If you have the strong foundation, setbacks will have much less significant impacts.

In chapters 14 and 15, we dig into some of the skills needed to prepare for success later on. Being familiar with the vocabulary here isn't enough. That's called talking the talk. You also need to be able to apply each of these skills. That's called walking the walk. And it takes work.

If you're sitting at your desk at 4:30 p.m. thinking, "Wow! I have a full day's worth of work to do tomorrow before getting on the phone," then why don't you just do it tonight? You might not know who they are, but there are people *consistently* working seventy- to eighty-hour weeks, acquiring skills that you won't get around to if your days are filled with catch-up and admin work.

Taking Vacation

You should take vacation. It's healthy. You won't miss much. And no one gets a merit badge for never taking a vacation. But here's the thing: you are responsible for a quota. Your role is essential to the company's ability to hit revenue targets. So when planning to take a vacation, it is critical that you plan for how you will achieve your goal, given your absence from the office. This plan usually involves doubling down on activity in the weeks prior, or having a clear plan for catch-up upon your return. You are not absolved from your goals just because you are on vacation.

Before leaving for vacation, make sure that everything is covered in your absence. A quick checklist could include:

* **Hot Leads**: If leads are in transit to the AE or might schedule meetings when you're gone, make sure someone can over-see them and make sure nothing slips through the cracks. Communicate the plan with both your manager and AE(s).
* **E-mail**: If you won't be responsive, put on an out-of-office message that includes the contact info for who is covering your territory.
* **Phone**: Change your voicemail to indicate that you are gone.

The bottom line is to make sure nothing gets missed and that you are able to fulfill any open commitments.

When you get back, debrief with whoever was helping while you were out and plug back in. Ideally, you don't end up pulling an all-nighter the first day back from vacation, though that will happen from time to time.

Maximillian's Mishaps

* Maximilian constantly checks email, text, chat, and social networks to see if he has new messages, which disrupts his day and makes for a complete inability to control his calendar and focus.
* Does not distinguish between what's important and what isn't, so things fall by the wayside, or he ends up making everything urgent and burning out.
* Asks co-workers to drop everything to help with items that are not important and not urgent.
* Cares more about his pet projects than his core job.
* Is constantly depressed since 98% of prospects reject him.
* "Forgets" to coordinate vacation with teammates and his manager, while also neglecting his quota and goals during the vacation period.

Boss's Brain

* **Impact**: Ensure that what you spend time on is designed to optimize your impact on current team goals. If you don't know… ask.
* **Employee Retention**: Demonstrate an ability to manage stress, execute on goals, and be a positive force on your team. Management wants top performers to stay and grow, not leave because of stress, failure, or burn-out.

Chapter 14

* * *

Core SDR Skills

Chapter Goal: Identify opportunities for improvement across several skills core to the SDR position.

*A*lex is not the most senior SDR, but she is the hero of the SDR team. Seriously, when the VP of sales wants to talk to an SDR, it's almost always Alex! Why?

* *Sales development managers and directors are not directly talking with prospects, and the VP wants direct-from-the-field feedback.*
* *Alex is the person on the team who demonstrates the strongest core SDR skills compared to everyone else.*

Yes, she is still learning, but she is well rounded and operates at a higher level than the rest of the team.

Sales VPs are under immense pressure to produce results for the CEO and board of directors. They (should) spend time focusing on the professional development of people on their teams, but when it's crunch time, the top players get called into the meetings, and everyone else is left behind.

The next two chapters outline several skills that separate top SDRs from the everyone else. Chapter 14 will focus on topics core to the SDR position, whereas chapter 15 will look at general business skills that also apply to being an SDR. Some of these sections get a little more into AE-land, but we thought they might be interesting to you as well.

Finding Pain

Lots of people probably think your product is awesome. However, no one will buy it unless they have pain.

Pain in business is much like pain in a medical context. It hurts. It's crippling. If not addressed, it can lead to other serious unintended consequences. As a result, it needs to be addressed.

Just as doctors ask questions to diagnose patients, salespeople need to get to the bottom of a prospect's situation.

Here are a few examples of pain:

* Our data is stored in several systems, and as a result, we can't create accurate reports.
* We are losing $400K/month due to rework.
* Half of our best engineers just quit, and we're going to miss deadlines.
* We are not in compliance with government regulations, so they might shut us down anytime.
* I am going to lose my job if we don't fix _____.

These examples, on the other hand, are not pain:

* It would be great to have a more modern user interface.
* We have a problem that, I think, costs us about $1,000/month.
* We're interested in seeing what's new and how we can improve.

If the pain isn't immediate and severe, there is likely little urgency to resolve it.

How Is Prospect Pain Discovered?

The bulk of pain discovery will be done at the beginning of the sales process via questions asked by the SDR or the AE, depending on how a company's roles are defined.

Imagine that you sell sales-forecasting software and are currently discovering pain from a prospect. You might ask questions such as:

* What are the challenges you face related to sales forecasting?
* Why is this a problem?
* Who is impacted by this issue?
* How long has it been a problem and what have you done to address it?

As SDRs ask these questions, they begin to document prospect pain and can determine whether or not the lead should be passed to the AE. When the AE speaks with the prospect, every conversation should discuss curing the existing pain, looking for additional pain, and leveraging the existence of pain to create urgency to get the deal done.

Do not be afraid to disqualify. Nothing irks an AE more than spending time on a call with someone who clearly does not have pain. Find out if it will make sense to engage with the prospect further in the future or if they would benefit from any other engagement (updates, content, and so on). If the prospect loves the product but just doesn't have pain, he or she might be a great referral source. You are asking for referrals when disqualifying prospects, right?

How Should Pain Be Used in the Sales Process?

When the SDR and sales team do a good job of identifying pain up front, it can be used over time to drive the momentum of a deal. For example, if a prospect says "this is a $200K/month problem, and if I don't fix it soon, I will probably lose my bonus this year," he or she has committed to a sense of urgency.

Reminding the prospect of this immediate and severe pain throughout the sales process, as well as demonstrating how you have a solution to solve it, can help a deal get done fast. If they have real pain and won't take a call with your AE, dig in and see what you missed, or find out if they have already selected one of your competitors.

Talking about Money

Talking about money can be very uncomfortable, but it's a critical skill for SDRs to master. Even if your boss doesn't want you talking about money with prospects, you will need to learn how before becoming an AE.

Prospects will use the fact that money is an awkward topic to their advantage. One of the things experienced buyers say to get rid of salespeople is:

"I love your product, but we don't have any budget."

Junior salespeople often take their word for it, sometimes even getting excited that "they love our product." Don't get happy ears!

If there is a real need and it's a priority for someone important, it is always possible to find budget.

Unlike when your parents taught you that asking someone how much they paid for their house is rude, talking about money is necessary during a sales process. Good sales methodologies have tools and techniques that allow you to discuss money in a responsible and transparent manner.

If money is an Achilles's heel for you, your sales career will be tragically stunted. Make your weakness your biggest strength by changing your personal mind-set about money, learning techniques for having open conversations, and bringing it up early!

Think Like a Reporter

When an AE prepares to talk to a prospect about budget, there are several points to uncover:

* **Who**: The owner of the budget (department and person/people).

* **What**: A range that can be spent to solve the specific pain that your product solves.
* **When**: At what point is the budget available?
* **Why**: Under what circumstances can the budget be released?
* **How**: How the budget becomes available (monthly ops meeting, and so on).
* **Risks**: If the company is not doing well, they may not be able to spend their whole budget.

This section could come from a book on sales or investigative journalism! While your company might not want SDRs to dig this deep before handing the lead to an AE, it's good to know these points because prospects don't always follow your plan. You may uncover the answers to any of the above questions during your conversation and be able to provide context to the AE.

When Should Money be Discussed?

Early. Period. While it might seem odd to discuss money before other topics, if the seller and buyer aren't in the same ballpark, it's a waste of everyone's time to continue the discussion.

However, discussing money up front doesn't mean creating a formal pricing proposal with terms, conditions, and so on. The point is to talk about roughly how much it would cost to do business together. It's perfectly fine to leave the specifics for later.

When discussing money, it's best to talk in rough numbers early on with something like, "Our product usually sells for $20–50K/year, depending on the package. Can I ask a few questions to see which end of the spectrum you might fall into?"

Common Money-Related Risks

Some money-related risks that can arise during a sales cycle include:

* **Willingness to Discuss**: If a prospect isn't willing to talk about money early in the process, there is a high risk that the deal will fall apart.
* **Approval**: Unapproved budget or the lack of a path to approval can kill a deal.
* **Release of Approved Budget**: Even if the budget is approved, if there are hoops to jump through to release the budget, the deal might be at risk.
* **The Entrance of a Financial Saboteur**: Executives with competing financial priorities might enter the picture and push against a deal.
* **Stalking Horse**: Some prospects have decided who they want to buy from and only engage you to have another quote to satisfy their bosses or to use as negotiation leverage with their preferred vendor.

If one of these challenges arises, an AE should speak candidly with the prospect and figure out what needs to be done to move forward.

Understanding Buying Authority

A prospect's buying process could be as simple as a single person signing a contract, or potentially so complex that it requires executive committee (or even board of directors) approval. During the sales process, you will want to understand:

* Who are the decision-makers, including who can say yes *and* no?

* Is there a decision-making committee? If so, how is it structured?
* How has the company decided to purchase similar products in the past?
* Who are influencers, users, economic buyers, ultimate decision-makers (big bosses), and saboteurs?
* Does the deal go to procurement after a decision is made? If so, do they try to renegotiate the deal to get more concessions?
* Who else is involved?

As an SDR, if you catch wind of any of these answers, it is your responsibility to convey this information to the AE. Depending on your company, you might be responsible for some, all (unlikely), or none of these points.

Why Is Understanding the Authority Structure Important?

Failure to understand the mechanics of how buyers buy will lead to the inability of your sales team to forecast opportunities. Additionally, overly cumbersome decision structures could result in deals taking several months, if not years, to close.

Imagine the following scenario where a sales rep (Jamie) has committed a deal to close this quarter, which ends in two weeks:

Jamie: Do you have any questions about the proposal?

Prospect: Nope. Looks good.

Jamie: So you will have it signed in the next week or so?

Prospect: No. It needs to be approved by the executive committee first, and they don't meet again for three weeks, then it goes to procurement for final signature.

Whoops! What is Jamie going to tell the boss? If there had been a better understanding of how decisions are made, the deal would not have been committed for this quarter, and the forecast accuracy would not be in jeopardy. Part of your job as an SDR is to have your eyes out for any information that can help to inform how prospects will make decisions.

There are Many Decision-Makers!

There are three types of people working at your prospect companies, those who:

* **Have No Power**: If this person said yes or no, no one they work with would care.
* **Can Say No**: Several people might have the power to kill a deal, or at least make it much harder than you think it should be.
* **Can Say Yes**: Might be one person or might be a committee.

Even if your contact can't say yes, they are likely important to the process, so find out who else should be involved:

Bad: "Who is the decision-maker?"

Good: "In addition to yourself, are the other people involved in this decision?

Think about decision-makers in terms of personas:

* **End User**: Will use the product once it's purchased.
* **Influencer**: Has the ear of the ultimate decision-maker. Maybe a subject-matter expert or someone with strong, relevant experience.
* **Champion**: Truly wants the company to buy your product. Champions can also be any of the personas on this list.
* **Economic Buyer**: Owns the budget that's used to buy a product.
* **Ultimate Decision-Maker**: The executive who oversees the purchase and/or use of the product. Likely delegated the evaluation process, but can override decisions.
* **Saboteur**: Does not want the company to buy your product. May point out weaknesses and try to kill a deal.

Discovery Notes

SDR discovery notes are a critical part of the prospect's buying experience. Consider the following scenarios that happen after four prospects each speak with an SDR for thirty minutes:

Prospect 1: Is then passed to an AE. The AE re-asks everything the SDR already covered, then sets a demo.

Prospect 2: Is passed on to a demo with the AE. The AE gives the standard demo, learning more about the prospect on the fly.

Prospect 3: Is passed on to a demo with the AE. The AE gives a demo tailored to the prospect's specific pain that the product solves.

Prospect 4: Is passed on to a demo with the AE. The AE gives a demo tailored to the prospect's specific pain that the product solves, but it turns out that most of what's covered isn't actually a pain point.

Here are the results:

Prospect 1: Will be annoyed.

Prospect 2: Will not understand the full force of the solution.

Prospect 3: Will have the best experience.

Prospect 4: Will be confused, and the AE will be furious that the SDR's documented pain does not exist!

It's OK to take rough notes while on the phone with a prospect, but they should be reworked for clarity and thoroughness before being presented to an AE. While they are "notes," they should be easy to understand and clear, not unintelligible outlines. That said, don't take an hour to write epic narratives.

Pipeline Management

Pipeline management spans from target accounts who don't know you exist all the way to customer renewals. Effective pipeline management can lead to revenue goals being hit or exceeded, while poor pipeline management can cause performance to fall short.

Depending on your company's sales strategy, SDRs might be responsible for:

* **Leads**: Individual people who have come inbound or who are targeted for outbound.
* **Accounts and Contacts**: Target accounts and associated contacts at a company.

Teams heavily focused on ABS will typically use the latter. Understanding that companies vary and you will need to manage accordingly, let's assume that "leads" and "contacts" in this section are interchangeable and are people who work at a prospect company.

The Lead Pipeline

Each lead should be assigned a "stage," which indicates where it currently sits in the sales process. While it's up to each company to create their lead stages, here is an example:

* **New**: The lead has been created by marketing, and no SDR contact has been made.
* **Contacted**: The SDR has reached out, but there has not been two-way communication.
* **Working**: There has been two-way communication with the lead.
* **Qualified**: The lead has been passed to an AE and converted to an opportunity.
* **Disqualified**: The lead will not be converted to an opportunity.
* **Do Not Contact (DNC)**: The lead has opted out of e-mail, or someone had a reason to mark them as DNC (because they are a competitor, for example).

When accurate stages are applied, reports can be created to help SDRs manage their leads and to give pipeline visibility to SDRs,

AEs, and management. You should have the ability to quickly and effortlessly pull up a report or view a segmented list by any of these stages, as well as other relevant variables such as "days since the last contact," "city," or "market segment." You control this world. Be its master!

Pipeline Math

Pipeline math uses conversion rates by sales stage to determine how much activity you need at the top of the funnel to achieve the desired results. SDR goals vary by company, but for this example, imagine that your quota is fifty qualified leads per quarter, all of which need to be accepted by your AE.

STAGE	CONVERSION RATE TO NEXT STAGE	CUMULATIVE CONVERSION RATE	QUANTITY REQUIRED
NEW	85%	85%	1634
CONTACTED	20%	17%	1389
WORKING	20%	3.4%	278
INTERESTED	90%	3.1%	56
ACCEPTED BY AE			50

Figure 14.1: Know what it takes to hit your quota.

Figure 14.1 demonstrates this concept by giving some example numbers.

* **New:** You reach out to 85 percent of all leads that marketing sends over. The others are disqualified because they do not fit into your ICP.
* **Contacted:** Of the people you attempt to reach, 20 percent engage in a conversation and are then marked as "working."

* **Working**: Once you have a conversation, there's a 20 percent chance they will be interested in your product.
* **Interested**: The AE will reject 10 percent of leads and accept the other 90 percent.

As a result, roughly 3.1 percent of all raw leads are accepted by the AE, meaning one of two things must happen:

1. You need 1,634 raw leads each quarter to hit your goal.
2. Conversion rates need to increase.

Build out your own spreadsheet and see if you can find a pipeline math formula that works for your business. Conversion rates vary by company, are sometimes seasonal, and can be unpredictable in early stage companies, but it's worth a shot to see if this tool might be useful to you in the future.

The cool thing is that you can then test hypotheses around lead conversion and use some of the "Other Prospecting Tactics" we covered in chapter 10.

Sending Information
Something you will frequently hear from prospects is:

"Can you just send me some more information?"

Maximillian would say, "Sure, I'll send it right over!" Bad idea. When asked for information, consider the following:

* Is the prospect just trying to get me to go away?
* Can I respond with a compelling reason why they should talk with my AE instead?
* If I do end up sending information, do I ask for another call to review?
* When I send something, what context do I provide in either writing or with video?
* Am I prepared to refuse to send information and push hard for a meeting with my AE?

Yes, your marketing team has prepared case studies, white papers, datasheets, infographics, and videos for your prospects to consume. However, between your initial conversation and the time an AE engages is not when you want prospects browsing these documents. You want them to talk with you, so do everything you can to make that happen!

Internal Q&A: Pros and Cons

Your coworkers are likely incredibly talented and have a lot to offer. They also have a lot of work to do, so while it's tempting to ask them questions when you're unsure of how to handle a situation, you should exhaust your own resources before doing so. Figure 14.2 provides a framework showing when it makes sense to ask questions internally.

As shown in figure 14.2, the next step after thinking you should ask a question varies, based on:

* How urgent is the answer?
* Should you already know the answer?

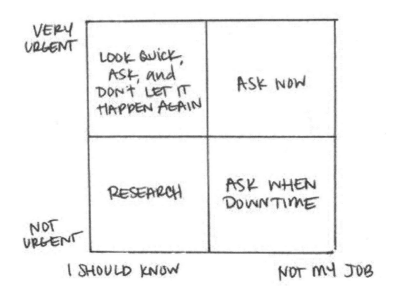

Figure 14.2: Know when it's OK to interrupt colleagues to answer questions.

If there's urgency, you need to figure it out ASAP and will need to ask someone. If you should have known the answer, you will need to spend some political capital and risk upsetting your colleague. One tactic for this type of situation might be:

> *"Taylor, I know we covered this topic in training, but a prospect is asking me questions about how foreign languages fit into our product road map. Do you mind helping real quick, then I promise I'll go back and review the training materials tomorrow?"*

If you own the fact that you should know the answer *and* show that you are willing to put in work to make sure it never happens again, your colleagues are happy to help. However, if you ask questions without putting in the effort, people will eventually consider you lazy and will become frustrated.

In cases where the answer is not urgent, put in some time yourself to do the research. Not only will you learn something new, but you'll also improve your research skills. If you can't find the answer after a reasonable amount of time, feel free to ask someone; just don't interrupt their day.

You might be wondering where "importance" is in this diagram. Well, if it's not important, don't bother your colleagues at all...just research it yourself, forget about it, or *maybe* casually ask when there's downtime, such as at the coffee machine.

Developing Prospect Trust

Trusting prospects can help vendors get deals done fast. However, a lack of trust can lead to a prospect blocking access to key decision-makers or preventing deals from closing.

A prospect's first impression is probably established before you ever speak because they know what the market is saying about your company, your product, and your employees:

* **Company**: Are you innovative and building things people need?
* **Product**: Does it work as expected? Are existing customers satisfied?
* **Employees**: Is the sales team viewed as a group of trusted advisors, or are they peddlers?

Here are some tactics that can be used when attempting to build trust over time:

* **Exceed Expectations**: Make commitments and overdeliver. At the very least, don't fall short of expectations. They don't care that "my previous call went over!"
* **Be Consistent**: Avoid surprises, so they get what they expect. When surprises pop up, trust can erode.
* **Be Available**: If they have a question, be available to answer it. If the prospect's point person is unavailable, have a contingency plan that can easily fall into place.

Here are a couple of examples of using social proof to build trust fast:

Case Study: We helped Acme Corp. solve a very similar problem last quarter. Let me walk you through their case study to show you how we were able to help.

Press: Gartner rates us the top vendor in the market to solve this problem. Here are a couple of quotes from their report.

Personal Connection: I see you are connected to Sara at Beta Corp. on LinkedIn. We helped her solve a very similar problem, and I'm sure she'd be happy to speak with you about it.

Tough Prospect Questions

Some questions prospects ask can be tough to answer. Sometimes they are extremely direct, or they might ask something where you know the answer is something they don't want to hear. Examples of tough prospect questions include:

* Your ratings on [X Review Site] are lower than your competitors'. How can I trust that you are better than them?
* My colleague had a bad experience with your company in the past. What has changed?
* You don't have [Feature Y], which is a requirement for us. Should we continue this conversation?

These questions are challenging, but when addressed head-on can sometimes put an SDR in a favorable position to create an opportunity. Just because they are asking tough questions doesn't mean they don't want to do business with you.

Making Up for Missteps
When your company has had a misstep with a prospect or customer in the past, instead of being defensive, take ownership. Try saying something like:

> I'm sorry that happened. I'm here to help rebuild our reputation. I wasn't here when that happened, and a lot has changed.

Drive the conversation back to their pain and determine whether it makes sense for them to start doing business with you now.

Selling Vision
Selling vision goes beyond what your company does today and helps the prospect imagine what the future might hold.

Here you can expand the size of your market beyond just those companies who are a perfect fit today. Prospects will see an added benefit because early adopters typically have more substantial influence over a vendor's product road map.

Selling vision builds brand loyalty and lets customers feel as if they belong to something bigger...like a movement. For example, there has been a lot written about Apple's release of the first iPhone. It had serious problems, but the vision behind it was very appealing. This approach is similar to that of companies like Apple as they lure customers to buy products that are unproven but are working toward something great.

How Can Tapping into Emotion Help Sell Vision?

When customers buy a product, they often base their decision on faith that their life is going to change for the better.

It's important to touch on what their lives will be like in the future versus what they are today. What is the status quo, and how does the product improve it? Does the prospect have a compelling reason to change? If prospects don't see value, they won't engage.

As for emotions, they can have a logical thought, such as:

This purchase has a high ROI and can solve our problem.

Or be more emotionally driven:

If I make this purchase, I can be the hero who fixes our customer-churn problem.

While ROI is a strong selling point, positioning your prospect to be a *hero* will significantly improve the probability of getting a deal done, and will probably make the process easier as well.

Creating Prospect Urgency

Vendors want to create urgency with prospects so they can hit their sales quota. The problem is that prospects don't care about your company's sales numbers...they only care about solving *their* problems.

Therefore, the only genuine way to create prospect urgency is to demonstrate that you can solve an important and urgent problem. When trying to create urgency, always reference pain you previously uncovered, and highlight what will happen if this pain isn't solved, fast.

Setting Next Steps

Next steps are what will happen next: a meeting, web conference, offline work, or anything else specific. While this concept is simple, you will notice that the business leaders you respect the most always set clear next steps.

Good Next Steps

Next steps should be detailed and straightforward. In sales, always make sure to BAM-FAM (Book a Meeting from a Meeting). If you don't, getting that next meeting will take a great deal of nonvalue correspondence that wastes everyone's time. Try saying something like:

"After we hang up, I'll send a calendar invite for a thirty-minute meeting with Taylor Smith, your account executive. After reviewing my notes, Taylor will ask a few more questions about your business, you can ask any questions you have about our company, and we can then decide if we want to continue exploring a mutual fit."

This type of language clearly communicates your goals and mitigates the risk of the prospect becoming disappointed or frustrated. Also, if a meeting or a call is the next step, it should be put on the calendar. **If it's not on the calendar, it doesn't exist.**

Poor Next Steps

The worst next step is one that doesn't exist. One of the mistakes that Maximillian makes is he realizes that he doesn't have a good next step and then tries to fix that. Imagine how frustrating it is for prospects to experience the following:

1. They take time to talk with an SDR.
2. After the conversation, they move on to something new.
3. An e-mail shows up asking for them to take action (maybe schedule another call), so they have to stop what they are doing and do something that could have been handled when they were on the phone earlier.

The example above might seem petty, but consider the experience it creates versus your competitor who BAM-FAMed them. Little things add up when it comes to creating a great experience for your prospect.

If prospects do not agree to a next step, find out why they are hesitant. If they are not a good fit or have no interest in your company, don't waste your time. The best sales teams maximize their time spent on winning deals and disqualify losers fast.

Next Steps Outside the Sales Process

Setting next steps with coworkers is another critical skill that will determine whether management sees you as a serious businessperson or an unpolished junior employee. One specific area where SDRs can practice this skill is developing next steps coming out of one-on-ones with their managers or AEs.

Maximillian's Mishaps

* Thinks that learning ended upon graduation from school. It's all about execution now!
* Thinks that inefficiency or inconvenience are good enough reasons to pass a lead to an AE.
* Is scared to talk about money with prospects.
* Fails to understand complex authority structures.
* Has sloppy discovery notes that AEs constantly have to re-work.
* Happily takes on homework, such as sending information to prospects whenever they ask, without asking for anything in return.
* Thinks the way to create prospect urgency is by talking about his quota and timing.
* Fails to establish and agree upon clear next steps coming out of a meeting.

Boss's Brain

* **Productivity**: Consistently keep AE calendars full of meetings with quality leads. Period.
* **Administrative Efficiency**: Log good discovery notes, apply standard qualification criteria, and and document strong next steps to eliminate inefficient activity in the sales process.
* **Pipeline Acceleration**: Demonstrate responsibility for the top of the sales funnel. Without consistency in your role, a bottleneck develops in the sales process, which prevents acceleration down the line. The pace and volume of leads converted to opportunities is the difference between driving a Porsche on the open road and a Winnebago through the mountains.

Chapter 15

. . .

General Skills

Chapter Goal: Identify opportunities for improvement across several skills that will be necessary as your career develops.

*D*uring her first month as an SDR, Alex had short coffee meetings with every VP in her company. A mentor had suggested this activity and also suggested that Alex ask professional development advice based on each executive's experience.

During the meetings, Alex was shocked at the pure quantity of topics the execs said they needed to master to get to their current level. Many of the skills were even outside of their core job function and more general in nature. There were also several topics that seemed like common sense on the surface, but became incredibly complex once Alex asked a few more questions about the mastery of the skill.

As a result of the meetings, Alex now has a running list of skills she needs to master and periodically evaluates her progress toward mastery of each skill.

Soliciting and Giving Feedback

One of the best ways to rapidly advance in your career is to aggressively solicit feedback and improve based on what you hear.

Here are a few tips when asking for impactful feedback:

* Request feedback often.
* Build rapport with people from whom you want feedback. Establishing trust will make people feel more comfortable when giving honest and direct feedback.
* When you begin to hear feedback, go into "listen and process" mode. Don't take it personally.
* Always acknowledge the feedback you receive as valid. If you think the feedback is misplaced, don't be defensive or make excuses, or else the feedback will stop.
* Ask questions and try to learn more about why the person feels you did a bad job and where you need to improve. Your engagement will make you sound interested and like you are taking his or her feedback seriously.
* Thank people for feedback so they know it is appreciated and feel comfortable continuing to share their observations.

Without feedback you won't know how to get better. Without openness to feedback and a drive toward improving your performance, career advancement could be slowed.

Prospect Feedback

Feedback can sometimes be used as a gateway to a sale. One way to start a sales conversation is to ask prospects if they mind giving feedback on your product. If they like what they see, they will likely be open to a sales conversation.

On the other hand, if a prospect's encounter with the product wasn't great, it will probably waste time to start a sales conversation. Asking for feedback when dealing with new prospects is a win-win situation; it either creates a new lead or saves the sales team from investing in a bad prospect, while potentially adding to the product road map.

If they bring up feature requests, make sure you know how to handle the conversation before committing to anything. Professional buyers know that SDRs can't make any commitments, so be honest. If your company doesn't have a good process to capture feature requests and articulate them to the product team, it might be an opportunity for you to step up and be a leader.

Customer Feedback

SDRs likely won't be involved in gathering customer feedback, but it's important to know what customers are saying about the product. Find out where this feedback lives in your company and make friends. In some organizations it takes a while to create formal case studies and white papers, so anecdotal feedback can be really valuable.

If customers love your product, tell those stories while talking to prospects. If customers hate your product, it might be time to look for another job!

Giving Feedback

Just because you are in a junior role doesn't mean you don't have valuable feedback to offer. When concerns arise, don't let them linger; face the problem head-on and as soon as possible. If you wait, your manager or teammates might be upset that you didn't bring it up earlier.

To ensure that your feedback is relevant and useful, be very specific and offer thoughtful suggestions for improvement.

Critique the play, not the player: "It was difficult for me to identify the most important points quickly from these discovery call notes," versus, "You suck at taking discovery call notes," is completely different feedback.

As an SDR, it's also best to make sure all negative feedback is given in private.

* *Never* throw your teammates under the bus.
* *Never* make your boss look bad in public...unless you are prepared to get fired.

Seriously, even seemingly minor complaints about your boss can cause major issues for you and demonstrate a lack of maturity.

Utilizing Feedback

Once you have collected feedback, it's time to put it into action. Some ideas to take action include:

* **Make a Plan**: What will you do with the feedback?
* **Share the Plan**: Create some accountability.
* **Monitor Progress**: Is the plan progressing?
* **Request More Feedback**: Are you improving?

* **Cloze the Loop**: Make sure the person who provided feedback knows that you took it seriously and that it's having an impact.

Ethical Dilemmas

Ethical dilemmas force you to choose between doing the "right thing" and something that may be unethical but has a positive reward (monetary or otherwise). For example, if a prospect says he or she will take a demo with your AE if you promise that [Feature X] will be built in two months, but you know it will take six months, it's unethical to lie just to schedule a meeting.

Ethical decisions will follow you for your entire career, and bad moves will hurt your reputation with customers, coworkers, and other people with whom you interact. In severe cases, a wrong choice may hurt your ability to get a job in the future.

Common SDR Dilemmas

There are several common sources of ethical dilemmas, including:

* **Overselling Product Features**: Stating the product does something that it doesn't.
* **Compensation**: If you get paid on leads that are accepted by the AEs, don't coerce them into accepting leads they shouldn't. Also, don't cut side deals with AEs without disclosing them to your manager.
* **Documentation**: If it's not true, don't write it down in the CRM or anywhere else.

Dealing with Ethical Situations

Sometimes an ethical dilemma will involve senior coworkers or prospects. In these cases, it can be tough to refuse their request. Just remember that following them down an unethical path can have negative consequences for both of you. In cases like these, the following guidelines can help:

* **Honesty is the best policy.** Describing how you feel directly is better than beating around the bush. Phrases like, "that makes me uncomfortable because..." can help articulate your position.
* **The other person has likely been in your position before.** After acknowledging your discomfort, see if you can get them to empathize with your perspective.
* **Avoid placing blame.** Even in cases where someone directly and knowingly prompts you to do something unethical, be soft in your response. Getting aggressive about legal or other consequences can result in the other party getting defensive.
* **Raise the flag.** If there is a situation beyond your comfort zone, bring it up to your manager, and do so sooner rather than later.

Saying No or NO!

Saying no can be hard for some people, especially at work. Saying no to prospects or executives can be even more difficult. There will be times, however, where knowing how and when to say no can save your job.

Though daunting, saying no gets more comfortable the more times you do it. Keep in mind, though, that when you are working with someone regularly, you do need to manage and limit the number of times you say no in a way that could hurt them.

Make it clear that you're busy with high-value, productive work without diminishing what is being asked of you. Having a sense of empathy for the person you're telling no to will go a long way. Offer an alternative, like suggesting a different deadline or sending them to a coworker who may be able to help if you can't. Just be practical and defend your interests.

Telling a Prospect No

One of the hardest things an SDR can do is tell a prospect no. Some common times where no is the appropriate response include:

* **Feature Requests**: Some prospects ask for features that are not a priority for your company.
* **Price Concessions**: Vendors often have pricing guidelines that cannot be broken, and even if they do, it's not the SDR's job to make these concessions.
* **Support**: If a prospect requests 24/7 support, it might be impossible or cost prohibitive.
* **Customer References**: It's common to provide customer references to prospects, but not until the end of the sales process.

When telling a prospect no, it's important to soften the response as much as possible. Some examples are outlined in figure 15.1.

Pitching Ideas Internally

Over the course of your career, you will need to be able to come up with and pitch your own projects. Successfully communicating ideas exhibits creativity and leadership skills, while offering opportunities for personal and professional growth.

Good Idea	Bad Idea
I checked with the product team, and while that feature is on our road map, it looks like it won't be built until late next quarter at the earliest.	That feature isn't a priority for us right now.
We might be able to reduce our price, but I'm going to have to let you speak with Jamie, your account executive, who can work with you here. When is a good time to schedule a call?	The price is the price.
Typically, a customer reference is the last step in our sales process. If it looks like our product is a good fit and we agree on terms, I'm happy to move forward with a reference.	We don't offer references to prospects until we get agreement to move forward from a decision-maker.

Figure 15.1: Use tact when telling a prospect no.

As employees move up in a company, they are awarded new levels of responsibility, including the opportunity to lead their projects. What all of these situations have in common is that projects need to be approved by management before anything can move forward. In each case, a strong pitch will encourage approval and leave a lasting impression on the executive. Being confident about pitching your projects will likely result in you doing more work you enjoy.

Preparing Your Pitch

The first thing you need for any pitch is a great idea. When approaching the ideation process, it's important to stay original. Borrowing or stealing someone else's idea not only fosters ill will with your peers, but runs a huge risk of destroying your reputation. When coworkers find out that an idea has been stolen, the news will spread. Even if the most senior executives never find out, your peers will know, and the damage caused to your relationship with them will hurt you in the future. Maintaining the respect of your coworkers is critical to career success.

When given the opportunity to pitch an idea, your approach is key:

*   **Have a solid presentation**. Define your problem, solution, and a path to execution. Learn it. Diagram it. Create something that's presentation-friendly and easy to understand.
*   **Be direct**. Your idea should offer a solution that you can easily communicate. Show how your idea will cut costs, make money, or do something else positive.
*   **Develop a champion** who has a management or leadership role.
*   **Prepare for objections**. Understanding the pros and cons of your solution will help you successfully communicate and discuss your ideas.
*   **Get feedback**. Make sure to integrate what you have heard from others.
*   **Get buy-in**. Ensure some peers buy in to the idea before it's pitched.
*   **Be thorough**. Make sure that the executive sees your idea as viable in all aspects of its execution.
*   **Stay positive**. Bringing attention to a disliked or shameful aspect of the business can be useful, but make sure to tread lightly. You don't want to offend your audience.

Why is Working with Executives Important?

If you want to be an executive someday, it's time to learn how to work with them now. When it comes to forming relationships with your executive team, keep in mind that executives look for reliability, competence, and results.

Reliability

When you say you're going to do something, executives expect that you will follow through. If you get a reputation for being unreliable, they won't want to work with you. Instead, they will buffer your interactions by putting someone between you and them or even feel the need to assign a supervisor to make sure you finish your work. On the flip side, if you prove to be reliable, you will get more direct access to the executive, which can help fast-track your career.

Competence

No one expects you to be an expert in everything, but your executives probably expect you to know the fundamentals, like writing, using Excel, and performing your core job functions.

You should also be able to work with confidence and get things done without needing constant support or clarification. When you do need help, always propose a solution to get the conversation moving. Show your executive that you've been thoughtful and thorough before bringing up an issue. If you're off track, your executive can help guide you back in the right direction.

Results

Most executives are compensated based on their ability to achieve results. If you end up working with them, you'll need to align your interests with theirs and work toward achieving mutual goals. If you can consistently deliver results, you will have a huge fan in the executive, but if you continually fall short, your failure to perform can significantly affect your career trajectory.

Keep It Professional

Even if you have a personal relationship or frequent personal interaction, always keep it professional with your executives. If something fun happened the night before, don't rehash it at the office in front of others the next day.

Technical Topics and Technical People

Depending on your business, you might speak about technical concepts or might interact with technical people.

This topic is another one that contradicts how you were raised. In school, the best students knew the answers. When dealing with technical topics or technical people, it's *not* a race to know answers.

Is Your Product Technical?

If your company sells something technical and you speak with engineers or IT folks, you might have a little brain reprogramming to do.

They know you don't know their business as well as they do, and they know you're in sales, so you aren't as technical as them. As a result:

> *When speaking with technical audiences, be humble about your technical knowledge.*

"Fake it till you make it" will hurt you here, and will likely result in prospects who won't respond to your calls or e-mails.

Conveying a Technical Message

If you're reporting back to your team on a conversation you had, again, don't be a show-off. No one gets points for big words. The following approach might work:

They said, "[Technical Points]." I took that to mean, "[Your translation into simple language]." Does that make sense?

Your audience might get it right away (congrats), or they might require further clarification. One way to test their comprehension is to ask them to "repeat after me." If they think they heard what you think you said, you're gold!

Office Politics

Whether or not you want to participate in office politics, you will have to at some point. While politics typically have a negative connotation in a work setting, there are positive ways that you can help others to advance the interests of both yourself and the company. Here are some examples of political situations:

Good Politics	Bad Politics
Creating opportunities to showcase your work to senior executives.	Stealing ideas from others and presenting them as your own.
Bonding with others outside of work to also improve your working relationship.	Passing blame to others for your mistakes.

Figure 15.2: Navigating office politics.

Get People to Like You

One way to get ahead at work is to get people to like you. It's not hard to be liked, and it can be accomplished by employing simple tactics such as:

* Thank everyone for everything and never be anything but nice outside of constructive feedback situations.
* Bring snacks occasionally.
* Engage people in communal conversations and activities.
* Ask people to lunch.
* Offer your expertise to people new to the company or new to their role.

However, it's important to avoid letting the social component overtake your work life. Most of your time still needs to be focused on contributing to the company's goals. In addition to making work more pleasant, having personal allies within your company can ensure there is someone to stick up for you when things get tough.

Managing Up

As an SDR, you don't want to show up for work, take a couple of breaks, go home, and collect a mediocre paycheck. If that were the case, you would work on an assembly line in a factory. Instead, let's accomplish something great, all right?

From time to time, obstacles will stand in your way, and part of your manager's job is to eliminate these roadblocks. Sometimes they don't do a great job here, or the manager might be the roadblock. In either case, you will need to "manage up." Some situations that might arise include:

* **Issues with Tools**: You don't have what you need to do your job.
* **Issues with Processes**: You might see inefficiencies or problems not visible to your manager.
* **Issues with People**: Don't be a complainer, but if there's a real people issue, bring it up.

Here are some tips for having these types of conversations:

* **Talk Privately**: Never have these types of discussions in public.
* **Have a Plan**: Showing up with a complaint and no path forward is not helpful.
* **Eliminate Emotions**: Being upset will distract from your ability to drive progress.
* **Think Twice Beforehand**: Is this conversation really worth having? If you're constantly ragging on your manager, you will soon run out of political capital, and that will tarnish your relationship.
* **Set Next Steps**: Commit to what will happen next and don't drop the ball.

If your manager pushes back, you might be tempted to go over his or her head. Bad next move. First, rethink your approach. The minute you go over your manager's head, you should be prepared to be fired.

Asking for a Raise or Promotion

The best way to get a raise or promotion is to negotiate for it in advance. Establish the metrics and timeline—then go perform! It's just that easy. You and your manager might agree on something like the following:

You: My understanding is that if I hit my quota each quarter for the rest of the year, demonstrate mastery of our sales methodology, and am able to get our VP of sales to sign off that I'm demo-certified, then I will earn a spot on the AE team in six months, correct?

Manager: Yes.

The problem is that few people do this. So you may find yourself feeling as though your tenure or performance deserves recognition. Here's how to manage that conversation:

*   Ask for a one-on-one meeting with your manager, preferably off-site so there are no distractions.
*   Outline what you have accomplished since you have been with the company.
*   Talk about your longer-term career aspirations and the role that your current company plays.
*   Outline your proposed next steps, which might be a raise, promotion, or lateral move to a different team.
*   Ask for feedback and listen!

Do not go into this meeting with urgency or ultimatums. Work toward collaborating on specific next steps and performance outcomes.

How to Quit Your Job

The cliché thing for us to say here is, "hopefully you aren't quitting your job"...but maybe you should. Figure 15.3 is our fun little "should I quit my job?" table. Obviously, adjust it for your needs.

TOPIC	IF "YES"	IF "NO"
ARE YOU HAPPY?	AWESOME!	PLAN TO QUIT
ARE YOU LEARNING?	SWEET!	STAY IF PAY IS GREAT
ARE YOU PAID A LOT?	AMAZING!!	STAY IF YOU'RE LEARNING

Figure 15.3: Should you quit your job?

Once you decide that you're quitting, it's time to plan your exit. If your job is tolerable, there's likely no rush, which puts you in a great spot. Your big decision at this point is whether to go straight to another job or take some time off and do something else.

Assuming that you're not taking time off, our opinion is that the first step is to make a list of amazing bosses you want to work with, either as your direct supervisor or as a senior executive. Attaching yourself to the right leader early on in your career will open so many doors down the road.

Once you find the right spot, give notice to your current boss. There's this myth of the "two-week notice," but we don't fully subscribe to that. You should give enough notice to fully transition your responsibilities to someone else. That might take two days, two hours, or it might take two months once you're in more senior roles. Just work it out with your boss. Often, they will ask you to leave pretty soon anyway, because nothing kills the buzz more than working with someone who has already quit.

Maximillian's Mishaps

*   Gets defensive when receiving feedback and gives aggressive feedback to others.

* Has questionable ethics, especially if there is an opportunity for monetary gain.
* Pitches incomplete ideas to management all the time.
* Crosses the line between social and professional with peers and managers.
* Uses technical words and acronyms to demonstrate intelligence and credibility.
* Calls out his boss's weaknesses in front of others.

Boss's Brain

* **Leadership**: Leadership is not a function of job title. Ensure that you demonstrate leadership by building and practicing the skills that lead to collaboration, professional growth, teamwork, and self-reflection.

Chapter 16

• • •

Working with Other Departments

Chapter Goal: Understand how to better support the marketing, product, and customer success teams, and identify ways they can help you as well.

Alex just broke a company record for meetings scheduled in one day, most of which were with CMOs in the technology vertical. She had recently asked the marketing team for a case study to fit this persona–vertical combination, and it started working right out of the gate!

> *Lazy Leonard: How on earth did you get marketing to build that case study, and why did they do it so fast? I ask for stuff all the time and never get anything.*

> *Alex: How do you ask?*

> *Leonard: I don't know…I usually just send them an e-mail or chat asking for what I need.*

Alex shook her head and went on to explain her strategy. Not only did she ask in person, but she showed up with a list of prospects she wanted to target, the reason current messaging was not resonating, an example of a current customer that a case study could be built from, and her exact outreach plan she would execute once the case study was published. Then, in record time, the marketing team delivered!

Working with Marketing

Marketing is one of the most complex departments in most organizations. You might have some or all of the following marketing roles or teams:

* **Content Marketing**: Develops written content such as blog posts, white papers, case studies, and so on. More and more they also develop video content.
* **Digital Marketing**: Manages digital channels and advertising, including social networks and Google AdWords.
* **Corporate (Brand) Marketing**: Promotes the brand through event sponsorship and general advertising, such as billboards.
* **Public Relations (PR)**: Works with press outlets to get coverage of newsworthy events. Also manages relationships with industry analysts.
* **Product Marketing**: Packages the product for sale, including editions, pricing, and messaging.
* **Demand Generation**: Creates and nurtures leads both online and at events.
* **Marketing Operations**: Manages tools and marketing-team efficiency.

What They Do for Us

Let's start with inbound sales development, since the answer is more obvious:

Marketing gives SDRs leads who are interested so you can follow up and convert them to meetings with an AE.

Ideally, your technology stack is set up in a way that automatically notifies you when a lead arrives.

You should also have messaging that ties to the Persona>Pain>Feature>Content matrix (the "Bray-Sorey Matrix") shown in figure 8.1 of chapter 8. It should help you arrive at the best way to open the conversation in a way that's relevant to your prospects and sets you up for success.

For outbound SDRs, the answer is a little more complicated.

* **Provides Messaging**: Another use case for figure 8.1.
* **Builds a Brand**: If people have heard *good things* about your company before, they are more likely to take the meeting.
* **Segments Accounts**: Work with sales leadership to figure out who to target, then make it easy for the SDRs to sit down and know what to do.
* **Maintains Data Quality**: If you don't have accurate e-mail addresses and phone numbers, good luck getting in touch with your prospects!

You know that marketing is doing a great job when SDRs can come into the office, call down a list, send out e-mails, engage on social, and then this activity converts into quality meetings with the AEs.

What We Do for Them

Your marketers are your teammates. In sports, when your teammate does something great, your job is to continue forward progress. If mistakes are made, everyone learns from them and gets better next time. The same principles apply to the relationship between marketing and sales development.

Inbound SDRs shepherd leads through the process of becoming opportunities. In an ideal world, 100 percent of good leads become opportunities, and 0 percent of bad leads are passed to the AE. Perfection is hard, and passing a bad lead to an AE here and there is better than disqualifying good leads, so don't be upset if you don't achieve perfection. As David Bloom says, "It's sales, not surgery."

Outbound SDRs leverage the messaging, positioning, and assets created by marketing to develop leads that become qualified opportunities.

Not all marketing teams have lead quotas, but they all should be aligned with the company's overall revenue targets. If there are not enough leads to hit these targets, that's a problem. Don't let the SDR team be the reason this problem exists!

The final point here is the familiar concept of clozing the loop. If something isn't working, tell the marketers. If something is working, tell the marketers! In addition to just telling them, provide some context, or "the why." Here are some good and bad ways to provide feedback:

Bad: Our messaging sucks!

Good: The messaging for [Topic X] seems to be confusing prospects. I think it would help if we adjusted it to [Proposed Messaging].

Bad: All of our customer stories are amazing!

> <u>NOTE</u>: Generic positive feedback is worthless to real businesspeople pushing for success.

Good: Customer stories X, Y, and Z are really working for me. I think they're working because of reasons A, B, and C.

Bad: We need better messaging for [Persona A].

Good: I'm struggling to convert prospects who are [Persona A]. They seem to only care about [pains they care about solving], which doesn't tie to any of our customer stories. Is there anything we can do here?

The better your feedback, the more help marketing will be in the future!

Potential Friction and Resolution

There is usually a natural and healthy friction that exists between marketing and sales departments. Ultimately, if everyone is committed to the company's success and is willing to put personal agendas aside, the best way to resolve any conflicts is to talk it out.

Here are a handful of reasons the sales development team might become frustrated with marketing and what you can do about it:

* **Messaging is not resonating**: Provide specific examples of what isn't working, as well as what is, and talk about it in person.
* **Not enough inbound leads**: First, get marketing's agreement that there are not enough, then work together to develop a plan to get more.
* **Too many bad leads**: Be specific about why they are bad and brainstorm ideas of what to do about it. For example, if most leads from webinars are bad, start there.
* **Content is too bulky**: If that three-page case study without summary info is not working for you, show them what is working for you and see how they can adjust current assets and future content production.
* **Prospects are confused**: If people think you do X, but you really do Y, provide *specific examples* to marketing and work together to find the root cause.

OK...now it's your turn to be the villain. Here are some of the reasons the marketing team could become upset with SDRs.

* **Poor delivery of messaging**: If you are not always on-message and crisp, the probability of converting a lead goes down.
* **Making up messaging**: Worse than poor delivery, if everyone is saying different things, marketing efforts are being wasted and the brand's quality in the market is being reduced.
* **"I forgot"**: Failure to follow up with leads will infuriate marketing. If there was a webinar, did you follow up with all of the attendees *and* the registrants who did not attend?

* **Asking for more without good reason**: Asking for *more* marketing assets is not helpful without describing why you need them and the impact they will have.
* **Sloppy hand offs**: If good leads are lost because of fumbles between SDRs and AEs, marketers won't be happy!

You're not perfect; we get that. But you can work toward not letting any of these things happen!

Working with Product

You might sell a physical product, a service, or software-as-a-service (SaaS). While most companies who have SDRs fit into the SaaS model, these principles can be translated to almost anyone in a sales development role.

What They Do for Us

While product management is incredibly complex, from the SDR perspective, it's pretty simple:

Your product team makes and iterates on what your customers buy from you.

Iterate is the key word here, as what you have today won't work for you tomorrow. Why, you ask? Customer needs will change as their business evolves, and competitors will take strides to steal your customers, so you need to keep up.

The other thing your product team does is ensures that what the customer buys actually works. Software companies typically have service-level agreements (SLAs) in their contracts that state how much uptime a product should have.

What We Do for Them

"If you build it, they will come."—Field of Dreams

Unfortunately, it's nearly impossible to attract a B2B customer just by building a product. SDRs play a critical role in helping make the goals of the product team become a reality.

Similar to the marketing team, the product folks will be happy when SDRs:

* Convert good leads to opportunities
* Provide actionable feedback

Feedback if the lifeblood of the product team. They are in constant conflict about what to build next, so firsthand accounts of what is and isn't resonating with prospects is incredibly helpful. As with all feedback, the more concise, specific, and accurate you can be, the better!

Potential Friction and Resolution

SDRs may become frustrated with the product team if what was built is not what the market wants. There are only two ways to fix this problem:

* Sell to a different market segment
* Change the product

The first option is much easier to attempt, so start there. However, as an SDR, it's not your call which market segments to target. You will have to get buy-in from your manager and sales leadership, but if you have some ideas, feel free to bring them up!

The second point is a huge endeavor, though it might be the right thing to do. Again, concise, specific, and accurate feedback is what's needed here when speaking with the product team.

Looking in the mirror, here are a few ways SDRs will frustrate the product team, as well as what to do instead:

* **Reporting bugs that aren't bugs**: A bug means the product does not work as designed. If there are ways to make the product better beyond what is built today, that's not a bug; it's a feature request.
* **Re-asking questions**: If you can look up an answer some-where, do that first before asking. Every second the product team is re-answering questions is a distraction from improv-ing the product.
* **Giving generic feedback**: Beating the dead horse here...be concise, specific, and accurate!
* **Junior-varsity activities**: Apologies for the generalization, but the product team is likely older and more analytical than the SDR team. The SDRs are likely younger and more opti-mistic than product people. Regardless of age, you are on the same team...make an effort to live up to the product team's expectations.

If you want to work for your company long-term, the product team will be a big part of your success. Likewise, you speak with more people than they ever will, so as their eyes and ears you provide incredibly valuable feedback.

Working with Customer Success

This team might be called customer success, account management, or maybe you have both. We are talking about the people who manage customer relationships after the initial contract is signed.

Of the three teams we cover in this chapter, SDRs are the most removed from customer success, though they both have a *huge* impact on one another.

What They Do for Us

Imagine that you are speaking with Prospect A. They have a very similar business to Customer X and Customer Y, two companies who have already purchased from you.

Keep that imagination working while thinking about the two following statements you could make to Prospect A and consider how they might react:

Statement 1: *"Based on what we understand about your business, we think we're a great fit. Our team built our product for people just like you!"*

Statement 2: *"Based on what we understand about your business, we think we're a great fit. Customer X and Customer Y are currently using our product to solve the exact problem you have today, and they have made short videos describing their experience."*

As an SDR, you might be able to convert a lead to an opportunity with Statement 1, but if Prospect A is actually a good fit, there's a *very good* chance you can convert them with Statement 2.

While the customer success team does a lot, farming zingers for you to use on prospects is the best way they will impact the SDR team.

What We Do for Them

Aside from having to deal with a product that doesn't work, nothing hurts a customer success team more than dealing with customers who are not a good fit. Imagine that someone on your customer success team has meetings today with two different customers:

Meeting 1 Goal: Reset expectations around what the product will do for them. They have buyer's remorse and don't know if they can actually use it.

Meeting 2 Goal: Review success to date and figure out how to scale to twice as many users over the next eighteen months.

The customer success team should be having lots of conversations similar to Meeting 2, and should rarely (if ever) need to deal with situations such as Meeting 1. The only way to make this goal a reality is to not oversell deals, and that starts with the SDR team.

If it's obvious someone is not a good fit, disqualify. Yes, you are probably compensated on quantity, but as you work to build your career and reputation within your company, quality is as important. If your compensation plan also contemplates quality, that's great, but many sales development leaders don't build quality into their plan for one reason or another.

Potential Friction and Resolution

You will become frustrated with the customer success team if you have customers and prospects in a specific market segment but relevant case studies or customer stories have not been developed. Since good social proof (case studies and success stories) are *the best* way to demonstrate value to the prospect, it might feel like there's a void in your selling process.

Depending on internal politics, you might not even work directly with the customer success team to develop these; maybe that's marketing's job. Regardless, showing "the why" is important. For example:

> "If we had [X Case Study], it would be easier for me to convert [Y Types of Leads] to opportunities, and there have been [Number] of these in the last [Number of Months]."

For these numbers to be significant, it's likely going to require pooling feedback from your whole team, so work with your manager to get things moving if you see an opportunity!

While it should not be an issue for SDRs, one way the sales team can frustrate the customer success team is by asking for an excessive number of references. Our position is that customer references calls should be the last step before closing a deal. Despite that, sometimes junior buyers who have little or no experience buying B2B products want references up-front.

If you receive lots of premature reference requests, the best thing to do is get some of your customers to record reference videos. This way you can use their reference at scale, and they won't get frustrated with frequent requests for calls.

Maximillian's Mishaps

* Argues with people over email while cc'ing several other individuals.
* Fails to understand how he can help other departments, but is always wanting them to help him.
* Fails to give credit when other teams influence his success.

Boss's Brain

* **Sales Enablement Ecosystem**: Do your part to ensure that a prospect-centric mindset extends throughout each department in your organization. Formally and informally, letting colleagues know when something they have done or created is having an impact will bear fruit for the organization and your professional relationships.

Chapter 17

• • •

What Does My Manager Do?

Chapter Goal: Understand the functions of an SDR manager. Identify ways to help support your manager today, as well as skills to develop if you want to move into sales management.

Awesome Alex rocks. That's why her name is Awesome Alex and not Average Alex. The other day, a bunch of her teammates were sitting around talking behind her back...as coworkers sometimes do.

Lazy Leonard: I don't understand why Alex gets to spend so much time with the execs.

Feature-Loving Fran: Yeah, they seem to like her more than the rest of us, even though I scored higher than her on the last three new product update quizzes.

Tool-Happy Terri: It's weird...I don't think she's friends with them. They don't go to happy hour. And honestly, some of the conversations I see them have are quite tense.

Leonard: Yup...doesn't make sense!

What her colleagues don't realize is that Alex has become a trusted resource on the SDR team. Her manager relies on her when front-line prospect intelligence is needed, and this reliance extends to many other departments within the company.

How has Alex become the face of the SDRs? She has simply applied her buyer-centric mind-set internally. When talking to prospects, she understands her buyers. Internally, she understands her manager and the other executives. She knows what they do, what makes them successful, and what keeps them up at night.

As a result, in addition to the time she spends working with prospects, she also gets the opportunity to engage in business conversations with executives across the company.

Functions of an SDR Manager

SDR managers are often the most reactionary individuals in an organization. They are constantly sucked into meetings dropped on their calendar by executive management, asked to attend "updates" by other departments so that they can keep their team in the loop, interrupted by "urgent" requests from their team, putting out fires with HR, required to onboard new hires, asked to sit on hiring committees, and so on.

The highly effective managers we have evaluated are adept at five core competencies: accountability and administration, coaching, mentoring, hiring and training, and leadership and motivation.

Accountability and Administration

The obligation of an individual to account for activities, to accept responsibility for those activities, and to disclose the results of them in a transparent manner.

Some areas for you to begin to understand include:

* What KPIs are your managers tracking? Why?
* What activity is measured? What results?
* What are the clearly defined and agreed-upon success outcomes and failure outcomes?
* What levels of mutual accountability exist? What commitments has your manager made to you?
* What is the feedback loop for reporting to your manager? Frequency?
* What meetings are you expected to attend and when?
* What are the leading and lagging indicators that will help identify red flags in your performance?

Coaching

Coaching is the process of building a relationship, ongoing assessment, challenging thinking, motivating, and driving results.

Areas in which your manager can offer support include:

* Developing your proficiency in your sales process and sales methodology
* Identifying gaps in your execution
* Ensuring that you ramp effectively and consistently hit quota

Mentoring

The informal process by which junior employees seek the guidance (by way of demonstration, explanation, or training) of more senior colleagues whose success they wish to emulate.

Areas in which you might seek mentorship from a company executive include:

* Learning company culture
* Becoming engaged with the team
* Your ongoing professional development and involvement in industry activities and associations

Hiring and Training

The process of recruiting, interviewing, hiring, onboarding, and ensuring that skills are continuously developed over time.

Areas that your manager may be focused on include:

* Adherence to an interview methodology
* Clarity in developing job descriptions
* Consistency and clear communication of hiring-process outcomes around company vision, role, and team
* Ongoing training programs

Leadership and Motivation

A constant push to increase team performance and help people achieve their full potential.

Areas that your manager may be focused on include:

* Establishment of mutual trust with you and team members
* Fairness in interaction with the team at every level
* Being dependable and adherence to commitments
* Being accessible both physically and mentally

Why Are They in so Many Meetings?

It's natural to look up one day and think:

"I've been sitting here grinding for two days, and my manager has just been sitting in meetings talking with people!"

While there's a chance that all of the meetings aren't necessary, think about the meetings that an SDR manager should be having:

* **One-on-Ones (Coaching)**: Ideally, they have coaching meetings with each SDR each week.
* **One-on-Ones (Pipeline Review)**: Bad managers combine coaching meetings and pipeline reviews. Since they're separate, that's more meetings!
* **Sales Leadership**: Coaching for your manager, as well as working on broader strategy.
* **Marketing Team**: Cloze the loop on what's working and what's not.
* **Product Team**: Report back on what prospects are saying about the product.
* **Customer Success**: Capture customer success stories to use in prospect conversations, figure out if there are specific

types of deals that have not been successful, and see which types of leads should be avoided in the future at the top of the funnel.

* **Sales Operations**: Review operational efficiency and address any issues.

Now maybe it makes sense that they are in so many meetings. Back to work!

Helping My Manager Be Successful

Let's give some advice that applies to sales development, but will extend to any job you have in the future. Helping your managers be successful is important, because if they see you as a critical part of their success, they will (want to) drag you along with them in the future. As we mentioned earlier in this book, attaching yourself to top-notch executives is one of the best ways to have a successful career.

When thinking about your managers' success, look at them as a prospect and think of yourself as the product.

* **Goals**: What are their goals? SDR managers likely have a team-wide quota, as well as nonquantitative goals related to hiring, onboarding, and training. These qualitative goals are called management-by-objective or MBOs.
* **Challenges (Pain)**: What's sitting between your managers and their goals? You are very well positioned to see if there is anything you can do to help, including hitting your own goals, coaching peers, or identifying process-improvement opportunities.

* **Opportunities**: What are some ways the manager can shine? What would need to happen for him or her to win "employee of the year?" Can you help make that happen?
* **Risk**: Is there anything that could occur and derail everything? Can you help keep that from happening?

The above points are abstract, but you should be able to apply them to your relationship with your manager. If you don't know any of the four points, just ask in a supportive way and see how you and your manager can work together toward mutual success!

Maximillian's Mishaps

* Fails to understand what management does, and unwittingly works against some of their goals.
* Distracts management attention away from helping the team and toward re-focusing him.

Boss's Brain

* **Alignment:** Demonstrate that you are working toward a common goal.
* **Personal Development:** By demonstrating accountability, executing on plans, and being committed to a process, you create a strong relationship with your manager, while also allowing your manager the bandwidth to become more effective. Their effectiveness impacts your opportunities for growth.

Chapter 18

● ● ●

Mentors and Thought Leaders

Chapter Goal: Create a plan to develop mentor relationships and avoid getting caught up in the noise created by "thought leaders."

*A*lex and her colleagues were sitting around talking about perfor-mance-improvement ideas.

> *Lazy Leonard: I think we should stop cold calling because Fakey McNameson said cold calling is dead.*
>
> *Alex: Fakey McNameson is a social selling consultant who is stirring up controversy. No successful VP of sales is saying anything about cold calling being dead.*
>
> *Leonard: OK, well we should make sure all of our LinkedIn posts have a teaser, are one line at a time, and tag lots of famous people, because that's what Social Posterfield does.*
>
> *Alex: Social Posterfield is a "growth marketer," and essen-tially a clickbait artist. Have you ever seen one of our buyers comment on that stuff?*

Leonard: All right then Alex, what about your mentors you're always talking about? What's their game and why should we listen to them?

What Alex has come to realize is that successful people love mentoring up-and-comers. These people are "paying it forward" and do not ask for anything in return, other than expecting that mentees will engage with what they say and push themselves to become better.

While the rest of the team is caught up with "growth hackers" and people pushing their own interests, Alex has surrounded herself with successful people who genuinely want to help her become successful. She knows that history tends to repeat itself and is on a mission to learn from others so she does not repeat their mistakes.

Creating Mentors

Mentors are created, not found:

> *A mentorship relationship is something that requires a bidirectional commitment over time.*

Asking someone, "Will you be my mentor?" is like walking up to a stranger and saying, "Will you marry me?" Try that and see if it works. Go ahead.

There are a few reasons why this type of relationship takes time to build:

* **Background is Critical**: The mentor must understand more about you and your experiences.

* **Test the Fit**: Just like a sales prospect, if the mentor is not a good fit, you need to disqualify and move on. It won't always be obvious at first glance.
* **Build Trust**: You will likely discuss sensitive information over the course of this relationship, so building trust is important.

OK, that's great, but how can someone come across a suitable mentor?

Finding a Mentor

As you begin looking for a mentor, here are some tips:

* **Set Clear Objectives:** Are you looking for networking opportunities? Do you want to learn more about your industry? Are you interested in general guidance?
* **Get Active:** Explore your community (physical and online) to find business associations, nonprofit organizations, college alumni clubs, church groups, and even network with family friends.
* **Set Up a Meeting:** After identifying a potential mentor, ask for a meeting and take this opportunity to discuss a possible mentoring relationship. This step is important and showcases your intent and seriousness. It also allows you to mutually agree upon mentoring terms.
* **Be Transparent**: Once you have found someone who agrees to be your mentor, make sure you share the same commitment. Agree on the schedule, availability, and context to avoid any mystification or resentment. Agree upon the topics you want to discuss, and keep your mentor updated on advice you have taken and applied.

Thought Leaders

You have undoubtedly come across many thought leaders (and wannabes) on LinkedIn, at conferences, and maybe even within your own company. These people are entertaining and offer the occasional golden nugget of knowledge, but be careful how much you rely on them.

Here are a few ways to segment who you should listen to from those who might do more harm than good:

* **Specifics or Generalities**: It's amazing how many "thought leaders" state basic truisms and are hailed as geniuses because they are on stage or have lots of followers. If they are not giving *specific tactics* on a topic, don't listen. Their favorite way to avoid specifics is by saying, "it depends" and changing the subject.
* **Relevant Experience**: Have they physically done what they're talking about? If not, that can be OK if they were very close to it, but if it's just an academic opinion, be wary.
* **Recent Experience**: For fundamental issues, recency doesn't matter as much. As we said in the opener, history tends to repeat itself. However, if technical issues are being discussed, things may have changed since they had relevant experience. Have they physically done what they're talking about in the last five years?
* **Practice What They Preach**: If this person is a cold-calling consultant, how many cold calls did he or she make last month? If it's a social-media consultant you're dealing with, is his or her social presence something that blows your mind? If not, move on.

There are a lot of thought leaders who can drive a ton of value, but be careful. There are also a bunch of wannabes out there as well.

Maximillian's Mishaps

* Sends messages to strangers asking, "will you be my mentor?"
* Believes anything someone with more than 5,000 connections on LinkedIn says.
* Thinks that growth hacking is the cure for everything.

Boss's Brain

* **Employee Development**: Demonstrate that you are on track to become one of tomorrow's leaders in your company by identifying outside resources who will be positive and supportive mentors.

Chapter 19

● ● ●

Career Path

Chapter Goal: Identify possible options for your career path and begin thinking about your longer-term professional goals.

W hen Alex was trying to figure out what to do after college, she had a conversation with a CEO that she still remembers to this day.

CEO: Where do you want to be in ten years?

Alex: I have no idea.

CEO: Do you hate talking with people?

Alex: No! I love talking with people and think I'm really good at it.

CEO: Do you want to be a senior executive one day?

Alex: Yes!

CEO: Sales. Start there. You will rapidly gain a ton of skills that you will need to be successful long term, and it sounds like you will actually enjoy it.

Alex: Wait, but you're not in sales.

CEO: I am. I sell stock to investors, help sell products to our biggest customers, and sell dreams to employees. All I do is sell.

He sold Alex too! From there she continued to have conversations with other people to work backward and determine some possible career paths. She learned that there is no silver bullet, but clearly, some options are better than others, and some are simply dead ends.

A Word on Sales Training

The best organizations we have worked with integrate training sessions into the development of SDRs, beginning with onboarding and continuing throughout the individual's growth at a company. These sessions may be conducted formally by using either external experts or internal trainers who conduct onsite sessions at regular intervals, or informally through team meetings led by peers or managers.

In either case, having trained hundreds of sales reps, here's what we have learned.

Academia vs. Professional Development

In college, time is on your side. You have a number of years to learn topics, theory, mechanics, and application before you are let loose into the wild to fend for yourself. Course structure is immersive, with a focus on getting correct answers and demonstrating knowledge.

As an SDR, time is not on your side. You have numbers to hit. You will be offered training that relates to your buyer, product, sales process, and sales methodology, then sent back to your desk to put what you learned into action. Courses will likely not be immersive, but rather tactical in nature. So how do you get the most of out of training?

Dive in and don't worry about getting right answers or looking foolish. That's the point! Fail fast in the training environment and during role plays so that you learn quickly, get repetitions, and are able to apply what you learn when you are back on the sales floor.

Be accountable by identifying a partner in the training with whom you will continue to work on concepts after each session to ensure that they stick.

Get uncomfortable by trying new concepts and new techniques. If something doesn't feel natural to you, it's probably worth trying and will help you distinguish yourself from your competition.

Finding Training Outside of your Company
If you are not fortunate enough to have regular sales training in-house, you will have to be creative in exploring ways to continue to develop skills. Since this book is in your possession, there's no doubt you're resourceful! Search your area for sales boot camps, sales training organizations, meet-ups, and other professional development

opportunities. Just be sure that whatever training you are receiving or applying is aligned with the techniques your manager wants you to employ.

SDR and Beyond...

Enjoy SDR life while you're here, but it's also important to think about what you might do next. If you aggressively learn the skills and concepts outlined in this book, you are well on your way! Let's take a look at some places you can go in the future.

Inbound SDR to Outbound SDR

As an outbound SDR, you will reach out to prospects at target accounts. Some companies start people as inbound SDRs then promote them to the outbound team. The logic is that folks with more experience are better positioned for outbound (prospects who don't know us) than inbound (prospects who want to speak with us).

Though you will still be an SDR, this move could be your first big step forward. Instead of just replying to people who reach out to you, you will need to strategize around:

* **Who** to reach out to
* **What** to say when you connect
* **Where** you should connect with them (phone, e-mail, social, and so on)
* **When** to reach out
* **Why** any given person would take a meeting with your AE
* **How** to move a conversation to a meeting with your AE

You likely did a lot of this work in an inbound role, but outbound prospects didn't reach out first, so it's much harder to get a prospect's attention!

Team Lead

Act as a player-coach where you still have a number to hit, but are also responsible for mentoring others on your team. A lot of companies have created this position to satisfy the rapid promotion demands of their workforce.

Do your thing, but we caution against getting too excited about a "team lead" role. You likely have some management responsibility, but no authority. If you remember nothing else from this chapter, remember this one line:

> Accepting responsibility without authority is one of the fastest ways to set yourself up for failure.

Additionally, the people on your team are your former peers, and even though you're promoted, these people still see you as a peer. You also have an overlapping skill set, so as soon as they learn from you what they haven't learned yet, what are you actually doing as a team lead, other than administrative work that your manager doesn't want to do?

SDR Middle Management

Here you have SDRs reporting to you, and you report to someone else who manages other SDR managers. A lot of what we said about the team lead applies to the SDR middle-management role, only now you are not doing any prospect-facing work.

The most positive aspect of this role is you get to coach SDRs... which is awesome! Aside from that, since there's a head of sales development above you, it's more of an administrative position than anything else.

If your company also provides formal management training as you're in the role, it might be a worthwhile stop. However, the amount you will learn here other than honing your coaching skills is fairly minimal compared with the rest of the positions in this chapter.

If your company has this role structured to focus any significant time on the following, be *very* skeptical:

* Chasing down AEs to accept leads
* Administrative work around scheduling interviews
* Creating slide decks to articulate information that's already written somewhere else
* HR paperwork and vacation scheduling
* Helping your boss prepare for meetings that you're not invited to
* Micromanaging the activity of others

Pure admin work! You have peers developing their skills and passing you by if you sit around doing this stuff.

Again, if you can get formal management training and you spend most of your time coaching, great. Otherwise, you might want to skip this role, unless you want to do these tasks and work your way up to head of sales development if that person ever leaves. You do you.

Head of Sales Development

This job has a significant amount of responsibility. You now report to a senior executive (likely the VP of sales or VP of marketing), you are the interface between sales development and other departments, you have influence over the tech stack, and you are responsible for building your team.

We're excited about this role because it's a true leadership position, but sometimes companies don't want it to be one. If you are considering taking a head of sales development job, make sure you are offered the following:

* **Formal Management Training**: Ideally from an outside firm, but internally can work if you have someone above you who has consistently developed great managers before.
* **Budget Authority**: You should be able to spend what you need to spend, as long as it's within a predefined budget. If you have to ask each time you want to spend money, run! You should also be able to spend more if it's not budgeted, as long as the investment makes sense.
* **Hiring Authority**: You will still need buy-in from others, but you should be able to make the final call on close hiring decisions.
* **Firing Authority**: If you don't want someone on your team, there needs to be a path to make that happen. If you have immovable dead weight to deal with, how can you be successful?

If it's your first time taking this type of job, it might be easy to concede on all of these points and hope for the best. However, if you can't spend, hire, and fire, then you're not really a manager; someone above you is just selectively delegating the things they don't want to do.

Account Executive

Close some deals. Make some real money. Now we're talkin'!

A lot of what you learned as an SDR can be applied here, but our advice is to make sure you are getting good sales training as well. Being told, "You'll figure it out" or "Work smarter, not harder" is not sales training. Neither is, "Read *The Challenger Sale* and do that"...good luck.

Remember what we briefly covered in chapter 2?

* The Buyer's Journey
* Sales Process
* Sales Methodology

As an AE, you will dive in headfirst here and master each of these. If you are able to find success, you will be a hot commodity on the talent market!

First Sales Hire

At some point, you might run across an opportunity to be the first sales hire at a start-up. This position can be amazing, or incredibly frustrating based on a couple of factors. The two things you really want to understand are: 1) does the company have product–market fit (PMF)? and 2) do the founders know how to sell?

PMF is somewhat ambiguous, but generally means that they are selling their product into their target market with some level of pre-dictability, and they have at least ten referenceable customers, ex-cluding their friends. Here are some guidelines based on these two important variables.

* **No PMF, no sales experience**: *Run!*
* **No PMF, sales experience**: Why do they need to hire instead of selling themselves as they approach PMF? They can hire an SDR to assist the founders, but not a "first sales hire."
* **PMF, sales experience**: Great opportunity, if you can find it. However, why are they looking at you instead of people they have worked with before? Be skeptical.
* **PMF, no sales experience**: Can be a great opportunity. Understand how they view sales versus product moving for-ward. Some non-sales founders think they are smarter than their customers, which will cause all kinds of conflict down the road. If they value magazine appearances over customer kick-off meetings, run.

In this type of role, you will likely report to the CEO and might also talk to board members, so mastery of the skills in this book is critical!

Marketing

Remember in chapter 16 where we outlined the seven types of mar-keting roles? As you learn more about each of these and gain more experience as an SDR, you might realize that shifting into the marketing department is the right move for you.

With experience talking to hundreds (or thousands) of prospects under your belt, you will have an advantage over many marketers due to your more in-depth understanding of what it's like to talk to a buyer.

Customer Success

In this role, you will work with customers and potentially carry an upsell and cross-sell revenue quota. First, let's clear up possible confusion between customer success and customer support:

> **Customer Success**: A strategic role that helps customers achieve the best possible results with your product. You may also have a quota around renewals, upsells, cross-sells, and the number of case studies produced.

> **Customer Support**: A tactical role that responds to specific questions and issues raised by customers.

While moving from sales development to customer success is not the most common route, we think it's a great move, especially if you want to eventually move into an AE role.

Starting in chapter 2, we've been consistently talking about the importance of knowing your buyer. The buyers exist in two states: before they buy and after they buy. There's a nuance here that you might have figured out, and while it's unpopular to say, let's put it out there:

*What do **prospects** do? They lie!*

*What do **customers** do? They tell the truth! The blatant. Cold. Hard. Truth!*

OK, so if one of the keys to success in sales is knowing your buyer inside and out, from which perspective do you think it makes sense to learn about them? In their lying state or in their truthful state?

If you have a top-tier sales training program and want to jump into an AE role, go for it. But if you are unclear how to best build your long-term skill set, consider a stop in customer success. You will learn boatloads more here than you will in an SDR middle-manager role.

Product

Most product roles require people with either a technical background or deep subject matter expertise, neither of which are common to SDRs (no offense). If you really want to work on the product team, a direct move is unlikely unless you work at a large company and are willing to take a very junior position.

Talk to people at your company and get some advice on what path you can take if you really want to work on the product team long term.

Operations

If you love working on process improvement projects and don't really like dealing with prospects or customers, a move to ops might be a great fit! As with the management positions, make sure you have a great training program and a good mentor here, otherwise you'll be spinning your wheels.

Almost everything in operations is a "solved problem," so unlike sales where you deal with prospects in the wild whose behavior is very unpredictable, ops is more about putting Legos together into well-understood formations to accomplish specific tasks. There's little wheel reinventing here, though you can still use creativity in terms of how well-understood principles apply to your company.

If you think you might be interested in ops, read *The Toyota Way* by Jeffrey Liker. If you love that, check out *Out of the Crisis* by W. Edwards Deming. This book is daunting to read, but Deming is the godfather of modern operations, so if you love this book, ops is for you!

Graduate School

Jobs like sales development offer a diverse set of real-world experiences that prepare someone well for grad school. Before deciding, figure out what you want to do long term, work backward, and see if grad school is a good fit. Again, talk to others who have been there and get some good advice.

Career SDR

Some of the most successful SDRs are not recent grads, but people in their thirties, forties, and fifties who excel at the job. With some SDRs already making more than $100K/year, the position should no longer be considered just an entry-level job.

Promotion Milestones

When it comes to promotions, there are two kinds:

Micropromotions: Happen every three to twelve months and result in a "cute" title change (SDR captain!), a small increase in pay, and possibly a small change in responsibilities. Micropromotions are basically corporate gamification to keep employees happy...don't get too excited.

Real Promotions: Happen every one to four years and result in a substantial increase in pay and responsibility. The pay increase can range from 10 percent to 50 percent, you *should* receive more equity, and most of your previous responsibilities are now handled by someone else.

When considering SDRs for promotions, management typically examines a number of factors, including:

*   Consistently exceeding quota
*   Demonstrating skill working with prospects
*   Mastering knowledge of buyers, competitors, product, and so on
*   Mastering the sales process
*   Developing sales skills
*   Leadership potential
*   Teamwork

General market conditions and other constraints may increase or decrease rates of promotion, so during tough times, it might be necessary for the SDRs to stay in their current role for longer than expected. However, if you perform well, you should still be eligible for additional compensation. Even companies in bankruptcy provide performance incentives to key employees!

Career Decisions

One of the worst parts about jobs is that you can (usually) only have one at a time. As a result, each career decision you make is fairly high stakes, so be sure you think them over carefully.

One fork in the road is when deciding between a higher-level position with less growth and a lateral move with more professional-development opportunities. The higher-level job might be better today, but neglecting to develop essential skills can slow your overall career trajectory. For example, there are some higher-paying jobs where there is no professional development; you are just contributing. Spending too much time in situations like these will result in your peers passing you by.

Additionally, at some point in your career, you will end up in a role that you don't like. Guess what? That's OK! In cases like these, the best move is to step up and have an open dialogue with management. If you're good, they will likely find a way to keep you within the company, since management is heavily judged on their ability to develop and retain talent.

Maximillian's Mishaps

* Assumes that his company had a dot-to-dot plan already in place for his ascension to the corner office.
* Fails to think about the short-term steps required to reach his long-term goals.

* Complains about the career progression of others on his team.

Boss's Brain

* **Keys to Promotion:** Demonstrate realistic ambition, the ability to develop a plan with management around professional development, and execute on your measurable goals.

Chapter 20

• • •

Figure It Out!

Chapter Goal: Prepare yourself to face any challenge that arises and win!

*A*lex walks into her weekly one-on-one with her manager, and to her surprise, the VP of sales is sitting there as well. She begins to get nervous and cautiously sits down.

> **SDR Manager**: Alex, today is a very proud day for me. I would like to thank you for all of your hard work, and congratulate you for receiving an offer to join the West Coast corporate sales team as an account executive.

> **Alex**: Wow. I don't know what to say. Thank you so much! I'm excited!

> **VP**: We're excited to have you, Alex! You know, we were not going to bring on any more AEs this year, but we just think you're a perfect fit, so we wanted to extend this offer.

As an SDR, one of the best ways to set yourself apart from the rest of the crowd is to "figure it out." Instead of telling you what we think, let's hear from some of your peers!

How Have Others Figured It Out?

We asked several current and former SDRs for some tips to help inspire your path forward. Here are their stories.

"As an SDR, I suggest making an effort to get out of the typical tech start up silos and interact with other departments. The career path for an SDR doesn't have to only be in sales. Getting exposure to other areas of the company will not only make you more business savvy, but it may also open unexpected opportunities that you can take advantage of in the future."

Sebastian Ibanez
Former SDR, ProsperWorks

"Sales has its ups and downs, so the most important thing you can do as an SDR is to get the right mindset. Do this by internalizing a story about why you're doing this work, how it's making you better, and what you do to win just by showing up. Having strong conviction in your story and learning everything you can from the people around you is the recipe for success."

Erika Davis
Sales Executive, Zillow Group

"The one commonality among all top performing SDR's is the discipline to apply massive and consistent action day after day, repeating the process they have known to result in success. Regardless of the emotions they feel on any given day, a top performing SDR stays focused and performs the necessary activities for success."

Justin Shie
SDR, Zendesk

"The biggest lesson I've learned in discovery calls is not to qualify leads, but to disqualify them. When you have this perspective change, your questions become more probing and can result in a commitment from the lead in following the sales process."

Deepak Annamalai
SDR, BrowserStack

"The SDR floor is a dog-eat-dog world. People forget that the most of the time, the SDR role is a consistent interview with management to qualify yourself for an account manager position. Those few calls you are too lazy to make at the end of the day are being made not only by your colleagues trying to leapfrog you, but also all of your competition. Remember that."

Ryan Imbriaco
Carbon Black

"Since the SDR environment can be competitive and (at most times) sink or swim, you need to look for ways to innovate in your role and iterate on your approach. Whenever I find a tool or methodology that I think can help me connect with my prospects, I try to A/B test it and compare the results. A few months ago I asked for my company to invest $50/mo. in a tool and now we're about to close a $100k deal with a prospect I sourced through that tool. This tool is now being used by others on my team and puts me in a place where leadership trusts new approaches I want to take."

Casey Schumacher
SDR, Skilljar

"Never make rules in your head for times, dates, or seasons that people won't answer. Your million dollar call could come at 5:15 pm on a Friday in December."

Brandon Hien
BDR, Map My Customers

"Be the trailer before the movie!"

Brian Vital
VP, Sales at InsideSalesTeam

"There are two keys to being successful in sales: attitude & activity. Every day I come in with a positive attitude, smile while I dial, and convey a positive tone across the phone. Along with that, I strive to not get distracted from my dialing. Every morning, for the first hour, I do nothing but cold call. This gets me warmed up for the day, the chance for great conversations, and also inspires my team to start dialing as they start coming in for the day."

Evan Satterley
SDR - TurnKey Vacation Rentals

"Understanding your role as an SDR couldn't be more important. It's easy to get lost in-between sales & marketing and not quite understand what your job is. Especially if you have never been exposed to this type of sales role segmentation.

Your job is aggressive awareness and education. You have to take these people from being completely unaware that they have a problem or who you are, to understanding it's an issue and you can solve it.

And if you're persistent enough, can learn from your mistakes, use your creative side, and continue to grind every day - you'll be wildly successful at this job."

Josh Schwartz
Director of Sales & Business Development

"At the end of the day, your main goal during a call should be to listen. Doing this allows you create a personal connection, which can help in so many more ways than just speaking about your product."

Jesse Darsinos
Associate SDR, Salesforce

"My success has been centered around a simple equation I developed called "the SDR Equation" which is simply Success= Work/

Time. Each piece is dependent on the other. Without time management, your work is pointless. Without good work ethic, your time is wasted. And with pointless work and wasted time, you won't have success. If you want to be successful as an SDR, then do the following: Work hard, learn everything you can, and schedule your day."

Matt Reuter
Team Lead, Sales Development

"Invest in yourself. The skills and knowledge you learn as an SDR make all the difference regardless of what career path you follow. Work hard and work smart. You would be surprised how many of your peers don't. This investment will create an advantage for you down the road."

Seth Olsen
Enterprise Account Executive, MicroStrategy

"When I first started as an SDR, I wish I knew that there is nothing to be scared of on the other side of the phone. Realizing that and embracing rejection helped my production immensely. I would listen to recordings of my worst calls and try to realize from their point of view what made them get off the phone, and then work to correct it on the next call. For future SDRs, soak up as much information as possible from the experienced members of your team and realize coachability will be the biggest aspect that will set you apart from your peers."

Zack Adams
SDR, Barkly

"Move Out Of Your Comfort Zone. You Can Only Grow If You Are Willing To Feel Awkward And Uncomfortable When You Try Something New."- Brian Tracy

Mike Yerke
SDR, Box

"One of the biggest things that many SDR forget is they are the first point of contact any prospect has with their company. They are the most effective, important and visible piece of any organization and often times the reason a deal gets kicked off or never leaves the ground. This seems obvious, but it is one of the things that most SDR forget- that they are truly the most important spokesperson in any organization and are the key to opening the doors that no one knew existed before the SDR uncovered it."

Jessica Nelson
Sales Development Manager, Sprout Social

"Take networking seriously and never write someone off because of their current title. You never know who will make the next intro- duction or where that person will be in 20 years."

Daniel Brigham
Director of SMB

"Outwork the person next to you and you will always find success. When I started as an SDR, if the others were making 50 calls a day, I was making 100. When we ran out of call rooms, I sat in the kitchen and made cold calls for everybody to hear. I did this in the first month I was an SDR, fresh out of college. I'm sure that on some of the calls I blew it-- but I grew so quickly from doing this."

Tucker Hood
Account Executive, Sigstr

"One of the hardest asks made of SDRs early in their careers, is to expect them to be experts in their clients' business. While I was growing my understanding of the business world as an SDR and where me and the product I sold fit in, the thing I found that I could always control was my level of activity. Not just how many voice-mails I could pump out - but a couple extra minutes of research, a couple of extra contacts at a target company added to Salesforce, a couple of extra emails before lunch and before leaving for the day, and yes, a couple more calls helped me separate myself from my peers, and stand out with prospects."

Matt McGowan
New Business, Plaid

"Think motivation is what is holding your sales team back? The reality is that kids look for motivation, adults just go to work.

Your job as a sales manager is to use data to inform coaching and then actually go do it. The data informs how you coach, but skillful coaching is what makes people great. Remember - your team's results are a reflection on you. You are who you hire."

Chris Bryson
Head of North American Sales Development, SmartRecruiters

"If you have ever golfed on a new course, you understand the value of a caddy. A caddy has put in the time on the course to know exactly what is necessary for a successful day. They know the distance, the terrain, and most importantly…they know which iron to use in the given circumstance. That's how I see my role as an SDR. I want to know the potential client so well, that I will surely set up my AE for success."

Aaron Cramer
SDR, Square Inc.

"Intent is everything. Prospects don't expect you to know all the answers, they expect you to be honest with them. Polished delivery or high activity are ineffective in the absence of demonstrating true, honest intent. Show a prospect good intent, and you'll win the relationship as well as the business."

Mike Ebbers
Regional Account Executive, BlueCat

"Want to blow our your number? Invest time becoming an expert in the space that you are selling into. Sales IQ, emotional IQ, and product knowledge are all vital - industry knowledge sets you apart from the rest of the pack."

Michael D. Bullard
Mid-Market Account Executive @ Lever (founding member of the SDR org @ Lever)

"Never conform to the status quo. If your entire team is doing one thing, make sure to do that and more. The people who will really be trusted to lead a Sales Development Team or get promoted to closing roles are those who aren't just following instructions, but thinking outside of the box on how they can be performing better than the rest. Social media, cold calling, and emails are all strong ways to build connections -- make sure to use all three."

Krishan Patel
Account Executive, ZenProspect

"The most important thing that I have learned as an SDR is to never be satisfied with what you already know. If I could give one piece of advice for future SDRs, it would be to invest in your knowledge because it is one of our greatest assets in the career world."

Kimmie Kreuzberger
SDR, Kentik

"In order to be a successful SDR, you need thick skin and the ability to listen and learn."

David Franklin
SDR, Agility Recovery

"Network with others early in your career and often. The compounding effect it can have on your career path can be incredibly beneficial down the road."

Matt Adler
Sr. Managing Dir, formerly with Nasdaq

"My advice to SDRs is to always focus your messaging around how your product or service will benefit prospects. It's easy to be excited about how great your product is and talk about all of the features and functions that differentiate it from competitors. At the end of the day, prospects care about how it will benefit them, and the most successful SDRs are great at painting that picture."

Dominique Catabay
Former SDR, DiscoverOrg

"My advice to future SDRs is to 1) Put in the work—get to the office before everyone else 2) Stay organized—record and automate what you can so you don't have to rely on memory and 3) Don't harp on mistakes—you didn't fail, you learned something, and there are more fish in the sea!"

Reid Anderson
SDR, PandaDoc

"The greatest challenge, but most important asset as an SDR is learning to strike your own balance between science and creativity, automation and personalization, technology and humanity. Use the templates that convert, but make sure they feel authentically you. Learn the workflows of the pros, but adjust them to fit your flow. Buyers don't want to engage with a robot, so always be thoroughly, unabashedly human."

Kasey Jones
Head of Growth at RevDev.io

"I was in a situation at a start-up where my sales territory had zero inbound leads, and I was held to the same quota as my team members, many of whom were living off of 100% inbound leads.

At first, I thought this was really unfair and I was angry, but then I decided to use this as an opportunity for growth. I made an educational video about my product that went viral on LinkedIn, and as a result, many of my prospects started connecting with me. This strategy is how I turned my outbound leads into inbound leads, and also ended up opening many opportunities for myself that I never would have had if I hadn't been faced with overcoming this challenge."

Kate Turchin
SDR, Evident.io

"Pull calls and have a 1:1 with your manager. As an SDR, this could be a little frightening, but your effort to improve won't go unnoticed, and you'll be amazed how much better you'll be a couple of months down the line!"

Andrew Zimmerman
Team Lead of Sales Development, Yotpo

"If you want to be on top of your game, it's paramount to know what the best players in the game know or follow.

I'd connect to the best SDR's on LinkedIn & request for a 30 minutes chat to share the best practices. Four such conversations a month were pure gold which you won't find in any book or a post. Plus the relationship you will build will go a long way."

Rahul Wadhwa
Sales Development Manager, Whatfix

"The #1 thing that led to my success as an SDR is staying curious. Stay current in the industry, ask a lot of relevant questions, and take advantage of every single conversation. Just because you called the wrong person doesn't mean they can't help you."

Lihea Choe
SDR Lead, Conversica

"I wish I would have known about LinkedIn Sales Navigator when I was looking for my 1st SDR job out of school. I was filling out job applications left and right like everyone else. It was very time-consuming. When it came time to look for my second job, I used LinkedIn Sales Navigator. It was a lot more efficient, and I filled significantly fewer applications."

Brandon Etra
SDR at Spark Hire

"Consistency and Honesty are critical. Always be willing to do the work, even if you don't agree. Work the plan daily and be totally honest and open with your team, your manager, your customers, and especially yourself. Feel great about the hard work and that you have done it honestly-don't worry about anybody else."

Macky Bradley
SDR & Social Media Ambassador, HotSchedules

"If you're an SDR, there is a ton of content out there, this book included, for you to learn, practice, develop and grow into a reputable SDR.

However, the one item that many people forget is that Sales and Sales Development do not come with a "One Size Fits All" methodology.

Focus on learning as much as possible from as many different sources as possible, and then create a Sales Development and Prospecting style that's unique to you and your company.

There's a gazillion SDRs out there reaching out to the same accounts. These are people with products just like yours. You won't be able to stand out by being just like them.

You have to stand out to be outstanding."

Saket Kumar
Vyve

Chapter 21

● ● ●

Conclusion

Chapter Goal: End on a high note and go practice what you have learned!

An SDR we know recently remarked:

"You learn more in the first quarter of working than you learn during four years of college!"

It's hard to argue with that, at least within the context of what you actually want to do with your life. However, since you took the initiative to read this book, you might adjust this statement to read:

"Now that I've read insights from two guys who have been SDRs, managed SDR teams, trained hundreds of SDRs, and consulted to hypergrowth companies as they scaled sales development, I'm ready to deliver some incredible results!"

It's your turn now. You won't become the world's best SDR just because you finished this book, but you took a huge leap forward.

Sales Development

We recommend that you continue to use what you learned here as a reference guide and periodically examine where you're making progress as well as opportunities for improvement.

The cool thing is that a lot of these principles extend well beyond sales development and will serve you well throughout your career.

It's also important that you apply these lessons to you as you see fit. We're not your dad—we're not here to tell you what to do. We're also not your "cool uncle" who uses shock humor and questionable tactics to make you think we're awesome. How many f-bombs were in this book? That's not the game we're playing.

Think of us as your big brothers. We want you to succeed. We will show you the way. However, if you insist on doing your own thing, that's cool with us. You do you.

Oh, and when you write your book, let us know. We'll buy it!

Afterword

What does it take to be a great SDR?

I've spent the last decade building inside sales teams at early stage startups, and no role is more important in the modern sales organization than that of the sales development representative. The hires made on a sales development team are going to be the first point of contact with prospective customers and will have a significant impact on the entire sales organization's ability to have enough pipeline to make its numbers month-over-month.

This role also serves the purpose of being a significant source of future sales, marketing, and other talent within an organization. Future executives, having started by hustling to bring in new business and therefore understanding market challenges and how the company's product or service is impacts customers, will create a company culture that thrives.

So what makes a rock star SDR?

While great SDRs come from a variety of backgrounds and personality traits, the best have a few things in common:

#1 - Cognitive Ability - They must be smart. Gone are the days of "coin-operated" sales reps who are strictly money-motivated. Today, an SDR must be able to solve problems on their own and be quick on their feet. The market changes quickly, new competition sweeps in, new technologies emerge to help accelerate sales velocity, new policies can require an entirely new sales engagement strategy...the list goes on. Rock stars have the ability to quickly learn, adapt, and execute without a tremendous amount of oversight and ongoing reinforcement. Show them once, and they understand.

#2 - Curiosity - Being smart is not enough, they must have a growth mindset and have a thirst for learning and growing on their own. Management cannot be on top of every change in the market, know every new competitor that might be creeping into a niche, and cannot stay on top of solutions or processes that might help save time and increase sales velocity. Rock star sales development reps take the time to learn about the market, get excited about innovation in the role, and are not resistant to trying new tactics to gain an edge and "level-up" the entire sales organization.

#3 - Emotional Intelligence - like a homerun hitter in baseball, success in sales development still means you are failing 19 out of 20 times, or more. As a result, you are getting your ass handed to you most of the time with prospects saying some pretty crude things over the phone, or via email. There are even cases of SDRs being publicly shamed on social media. It is a results-driven, high-pressure, "what-have-you-done-for-me-lately?" role. The top reps not only recognize and manage their own emotions, but also have the ability to understand and navigate the emotions of others. Being able to keep a positive mindset while simultaneously adapting your approach is crucial for long-term, sustainable success in the role.

#4 - Passion - This one is a game changer. The SDR who is smart, curious, and has high emotional intelligence will be a top 5% producer, however, if you are passionate about the product or service you are selling and genuinely want to help each and every person you engage with...then slap on a horn and call yourself a unicorn! You are a rare breed. These individuals make every person around them better and will not stop at "no," "not interested," or "not now." They find a way to help prospects understand why their company exists, the problems they are solving for customers, and most importantly, why a prospect should pay attention. These individuals understand the value of building relationships that last for years to come.

Ryan Reisert

Appendix A: Sample Offer Letter

[Company Logo]

[Date]

[Your Name]

Offer of Employment

Dear [Your Name]:

As the Director of Sales Development of [Company Name], one of my favorite and most important responsibilities is making sure that our team is filled with awesome over-achieving people. I look for those with integrity, intelligence, an appreciation of team, and a proven record of success. I've had the belief that you are an "awesome over-achiever" since our first conversation, and I am tremendously excited to present you with an offer to join our team. Now for some "legalese" with the details…

[Company Name] is pleased to offer you the position of Sales Development Representative, on the following terms

Your role as a Sales Development Representative is to convert leads into opportunities for Account Executives to close. This may include inbound or outbound lead generation, as well as research. You will report to the Director of Sales Development. You will be primarily responsible for [Company Name]'s customer segment in the [market segment]. Of course, [Company Name] may change your position, duties, and work location from time to time in its discretion.

Your annualized salary will be $55,000, pro-rated to your start date, less all deductions required by law, which covers all hours worked. You will also be eligible to receive variable compensation payments based on your attainment of quota under the terms and conditions of the Company's applicable variable compensation plan. The variable compensation plan will set out target quotas, % variable compensation at different performance tiers, bonuses, and any agreed upon draw. Irrespective of the variable compensation plan, your total target compensation, assuming 100% of the agreed quota is met, will be approximately $80,000. The exact details of attaining this total compensation target are to be finalized in the aforementioned variable compensation plan.

Like all full time [Company Name] employees, you will be paid semi-monthly, and you will be eligible to participate in regular health insurance, retirement, and any other employee benefit plans established by [Company Name] for its employees from time to time in accordance with the terms of those plans. [Company Name] may change compensation and benefits from time to time in its discretion.

Subject to approval by [Company Name]'s Board of Directors (the "Board"), under the [Company Name] [Year of Plan Adoption] Equity Incentive Plan (the "Plan"), [Company Name] shall grant you an option to purchase [Number of Shares] shares (the "Option") of [Company Name]'s Common Stock at fair market value as determined by the Board as of the date of grant. The Option will be subject to the terms and conditions of the Plan and your grant agreement. Your grant agreement will include a four-year vesting schedule, under which 25 percent of your shares will vest after twelve months of employment, with the remaining shares vesting monthly thereafter, until either your Option is fully vested or your employment ends, whichever occurs first.

As a [Company Name] employee, you will be expected to abide by [Company Name] rules and policies. As a condition of employment, you must sign and comply with the attached Employee Confidential Information and Inventions Assignment Agreement, which prohibits unauthorized use or disclosure of [Company Name] proprietary information, among other obligations.

In your work for [Company Name], you will be expected not to use or disclose any confidential information, including trade secrets, of any former employer or other person to whom you have an obligation of confidentiality. Rather, you will be expected to use only that information which is generally known and used by persons with training and experience comparable to your own, which is common knowledge in the industry or otherwise legally in the public domain, or which is otherwise provided or developed by [Company Name]. You agree that you will not bring onto [Company Name] premises any unpublished documents or property belonging to any former employer or other person to whom you have an obligation of confidentiality. You hereby represent that you have disclosed to [Company Name] any contract you have signed that may restrict your activities on behalf of [Company Name].

Normal business hours, while flexible upon discussion with the Director of Sales Development, are generally from [Start Time] to [End Time], Monday through Friday.

You may terminate your employment with [Company Name] at any time and for any reason whatsoever simply by notifying [Company Name]. Likewise, [Company Name] may terminate your employment at any time, with or without cause or advance notice. Your employment at-will status can only be modified in a written agreement signed by you and by an officer of [Company Name].

This offer is contingent upon satisfactory proof of your right to work in the United States. You agree to assist as needed and to complete any documentation at [Company Name]'s request to meet these conditions. This offer is also contingent upon [Company Name]'s conversations with references from your past work and education experiences.

This letter, together with your Employee Confidential Information and Inventions Assignment Agreement, forms the complete and exclusive statement of your employment agreement with [Company Name]. It supersedes any other agreements or promises made to you by anyone, whether oral or written. Changes in your employment terms, other than those changes expressly reserved to [Company Name]'s discretion in this letter, require a written modification signed by [Company Name]'s Director of Sales Development.

Please sign and date this letter, and the enclosed Employee Confidential Information and Inventions Assignment Agreement and return them to me by [Date], if you wish to accept employment at [Company Name] under the terms described above. If you accept our offer, we will work with you to determine an appropriate start date.

We look forward to your favorable reply and to bringing you on board!

Sincerely,

_____

[Name], Director of Sales Development

Accepted:

_____

[Your Name]

_____

Date

Attachment: Employee Confidential Information and Inventions Assignment Agreement

Made in the USA
San Bernardino, CA
15 December 2018